Contents

Introduction

Introduction

A Lesson for Every Day: Literacy is a series of seven photocopiable activity books for developing children's ability to communicate with others through speaking and listening, and reading and writing.

The activities provide opportunities for children to read different genres, and to read fluently through using phonic knowledge of grapheme-phoneme correspondences and blending as their prime approach for decoding unfamiliar words. The books also help children to spell words accurately by combining the use of grapheme–phoneme correspondence knowledge as the prime approach, and morphological knowledge and etymological information.

The series develops children's understanding of sentences and their ability to form sentences, with activities that help them to practise their skills in organising and writing texts for different purposes.

The importance of dance, songs and rhymes is recognised in the development of communication skills. The activities provide or are linked to various games, rhymes, songs and stories as well as to familiar or everyday situations.

The books provide learning activities to support all the strands of the Primary Framework for Literacy.

The activities

To help teachers to select appropriate learning experiences for their pupils, the activities have been grouped into sections by text-type (narrative, non-fiction or poetry) and by genre. However, the activities need not be presented to children in the order in which they appear in the book, unless otherwise stated.

Some of the activities can be carried out with the whole class, some are more suitable for small groups and others

are for individual work, especially where the teacher and teaching assistants are working more closely with other groups. Many are generic and can be adapted; the notes on the activities in the grids on pages 6-24 and, in some cases, the notes at the foot of the page provide suggestions and ideas for this and for developing extension activities. Many of the activities can be adapted for use at different levels, to suit the differing levels of attainment of the children (see the teachers' notes on the pages). The activities can be used in connection with different areas of the curriculum, some of which are suggested in the notes on the activities.

The activities emphasise the importance of providing opportunities for children to enjoy novels, stories, plays, films and poetry – not just to learn about how they are written – and that children have time to listen to, repeat, learn, recite and join in poems for enjoyment. It is also important to encourage children to read non-fiction for enjoyment as well as for finding specific information.

Reading

Most children will be able to carry out the activities independently but some may need help in reading the instructions on the sheets. It is expected that someone will read them to or with them, since children learn to recognise the purpose of instructions before they can read them.

Organisation

The activities require very few resources besides pencils, crayons, scissors and glue. Other materials are specified in the teachers' notes on the pages: for example, story books, nursery rhymes, an interactive whiteboard, audio or video recording equipment (such as a tape recorder, camera or mobile phone) soft toys, dressing-up items, information books and dictionaries.

Extension activities

Most of the activity sheets end with a challenge (**Now try this!**) which reinforces and extends the children's learning. These more challenging activities might be appropriate for only a few children; it is not expected that the whole class should complete them, although many more children might benefit from them with appropriate assistance – possibly as a guided or shared activity. On some pages there is space for the children to complete extension activities that involve writing or drawing, but others will require a separate sheet of paper.

Notes on the activities

The notes on the activities in the grids on pages 6-24 expand upon those which are provided at the bottom of most activity pages. They give ideas and suggestions for making the most of the activity sheet, including suggestions for the whole-class introduction, the plenary session or for follow-up work using an adapted version of the activity sheet.

Assessment

Use the completed activities as part of your day-to-day assessment to help you to build a picture of children's learning in order to plan future teaching and learning. Activities can also be used as examples of significant evidence for your periodic assessment. In order to help you to make reliable judgements about your pupils' attainment, the assessment focuses for each activity are given in the grids on pages 6-24. Some of the activities provide opportunities for children to carry out self assessment.

Encourage children to reflect on their learning and discuss with them whether there are areas that they feel they need to practise further.

The CD-ROM

All activity sheets can be found as PDF and Word versions on the accompanying CD-ROM. These can be printed or displayed on an interactive whiteboard. The Word versions can be customised in Microsoft Word in order to assist personalised learning.

They can be accessed through an interface that makes it easy to select worksheets and display them. You can also search for lessons that will meet a particular Assessment Focus for Assessing Pupils' Progress. For more information on system requirements, please see the inside front cover.

If you have any questions regarding the *A Lesson For Every Day* CD-ROM, please email us at the address below. We will get back to you as soon as possible.

educationalsales@acblack.com

Year 2 Narrative unit 1 Stories with familiar settings

Activity name	Strand and learning objectives	Notes on the activities	Assessment Focus	Page number
Say it with letters	**1. Speaking** Speak with clarity and use appropriate intonation when reading and reciting texts	**Say it with letters** focuses on speaking clearly and using intonation when reading. By using only the letters of the alphabet to communicate a message, the children, having no words to read, concentrate on expression and tone of voice. You could introduce this by playing a tape-recording from a foreign language radio programme in which an easily-recognised type of dialogue takes place: for example, a quiz, instructions, an urgent warning, a request for help or someone telling a joke or a funny story. Discuss whether the people speak quickly or slowly, whether their voices are loud or quiet, lively or subdued and so on. After they have completed the activity sheet, invite volunteers to demonstrate how they read each 'quotation'. The children could also 'speak in letters' to sound as if they are telling someone off, soothe or calm a baby, give a command to a dog, cheer a football team on. Link this with reciting poetry in literacy lessons. **Vocabulary:** expression, fast, lively, loud, quick, quiet, slow, subdued, tone of voice.	**Speaking and listening AF1** Talk in purposeful and imaginative ways to explore ideas and feelings, adapting and varying structure and vocabulary according to purpose, listeners, and content	25
It's my house!	**1. Speaking** Tell real and imagined stories using the conventions of familiar story language	**It's my house!** provides a picture story and invites the children to tell the story using the conventions of familiar story language. Ask them how it might begin: for example, by saying when it happened (One day, One morning, One afternoon). Discuss what they need to say next (who the character is, where she was and, perhaps, what she was doing): for example, One morning Emma was skipping when she found a big box in the garden. This could be linked with work on creating and shaping texts in literacy lessons. Encourage them to think of ways of making the story interesting: for example, through using dialogue. You could display the page on an interactive whiteboard but mask all but the first four pictures. Ask the children what is going on in the first three pictures and then what happens in the fourth. They should notice that two additional characters are introduced. Ask what these two children wanted to do and what they might have said. Then ask what the first character replied. The children could predict what happens next. **Vocabulary:** character, one afternoon, one day, one morning, setting, story, speak, talk.	**Speaking and listening AF1** Talk in purposeful and imaginative ways to explore ideas and feelings, adapting and varying structure and vocabulary according to purpose, listeners, and content	26
Rhyme characters	**4. Drama** Adopt appropriate roles in small or large groups and consider alternative courses of action	**Rhyme characters.** Some children might be able to think up rhyming lines for the characters to speak. You could model some examples: 'Humpty Dumpty sat on a wall / Little Bo Peep said, "Get down or you'll fall!"'; 'Little Bo Peep has lost her sheep and doesn't know where to find them / Get a sheepdog and the sheep will come home / With the sheepdog running behind them.' **Vocabulary:** act, character, rhyme, role, speak.	**Speaking and listening AF3** Create and sustain different roles and scenarios, adapting techniques to explore texts, ideas, and issues	27
Elves		**Elves.** The children could enact a story in which the elves venture above the floorboards or influence what goes on there (in helpful or mischievous ways). There are many possibilities of developing an adventure or suspense story. **Vocabulary:** act, adventure, character, role, scribe, setting, suspense.		28
Mr Dozy's hat	**5. Word recognition: decoding (reading) and encoding (spelling)** Spell with increasing accuracy and confidence, drawing on word recognition and knowledge of word structure and spelling patterns	**Mr Dozy's hat** helps the children to develop a concept of the past tense. The activity should be introduced once they have had opportunities for oral work on changing tenses. They could compare storybooks written in the present and past tenses: for example, (present tense) Ladybird Read-it-Yourself series; (past tense) The Tiny Seed and The Very Hungry Caterpillar (Eric Carle); (past tense) (present tense in dialogue) Can't You Sleep, Little Bear? The children could also retell simple present tense stories, such as fairytales from the Ladybird Read-it-Yourself series, in the past tense. Use the CD-ROM to produce a less challenging activity: you could delete parts of the text and enlarge the part retained.	**Reading AF1** Use a range of strategies including accurate decoding of text, to read for meaning; **Writing AF8** Use correct spelling	29
Mrs Forgetful		**Mrs Forgetful** helps the children to develop a concept of the past tense. This activity is intended to be carried out orally so that the children focus on the meanings of the words and understand why they change, in preparation for learning to construct past tenses. After they have responded to the questions ask them which words are different from Mrs Forgetful's sentence: for example, Today I am walking to the shops. Yesterday you walked to the park. Draw attention to the changed verb and introduce the term past.		30
Past endings		**Past endings** reinforces understanding and application of the -ed suffix for the past tense. The children learn to spell, drawing on knowledge of word structure and spelling patterns, including common inflections. Some verbs in this activity have simple past tense endings where the base words do not change before -ed is added; in others the final e is deleted first (taste, bounce); but the focus is on the sound of the suffix. To introduce the activity, say the heading words mended and crashed very clearly and ask the children to listen to the endings. They could also tap out the phonemes and write the words on a phoneme frame to help them to recognise where the -ed ending comprises one phoneme and where it comprises two. Other useful words include dusted, ended, hated, landed, loaded, needed, nested, painted, panted, pasted, pointed, raided, rested, roasted, sorted, sounded, started, tested, toasted, waded; and asked, baked, begged, bowled, brushed, called, clapped, crushed, curled, dragged, dropped, grabbed, helped, hissed, hummed, kissed, laughed, lived, loved, pushed, rained, robbed, slashed, smashed, snowed, stabbed, stopped, turned, washed.		31
Program the robots		**Program the robots** helps the children to learn to spell, drawing on knowledge of word structure and spelling patterns. It consolidates understanding and application of the -ed suffix for the past tense. From previous activities they will have learned that a past tense ending that sounds like /t/ is spelled ed, and understand why. For all the verbs in this activity the base word is unchanged before the -ed suffix is added. Some children might be able to identify the phonemes that usually precede each -ed ending pronunciation and use this to help them to predict the pronunciation of past tense endings for less familiar verbs: for example, conduct, exist, protect, remain, repair, restrict.		32
Base words with -ed		**Base words with -ed** consolidates the children's spelling skills, drawing on knowledge of word structure, and reinforces understanding and application of the -ed suffix for the past tense. It is useful to introduce the term base word for a word that can be altered to make other words that are related to it: for example, walk, walked, walking, walker. This activity focuses on verbs that end with e, which is deleted before the -ed suffix is added. Other useful verbs include amaze, amuse, choke, close, cycle, dance, dare, dive, fade, glance, like, love, poke, pounce, prance, slice.		33

Page	Activity	Objective	Teaching notes	Assessment focuses
34	Copycats		**Copycats** consolidates the children's spelling skills, drawing on knowledge of word structure, and reinforces understanding and application of the **-ed** suffix for the past tense. This activity focuses on verbs that end with **y**, which is changed to **i** before the **-ed** suffix is added. You could remind the children of their previous learning of the **ie** spelling of the **/ee/** phoneme (for example, *thief, chief, field* and past tense verbs such as *carried, married, pitied*) and of the **ie** spelling of the **/igh/** phoneme (for example, *die, died*, as well as verbs such as *cried, denied, applied*). Useful verbs include *bury, ferry; cry, deny, dry, fry, rely, reply, spy, try*. Note that a **y** ending changes to **i** only when preceded by a consonant (or double consonant). For an easier activity, use the CD-ROM to edit the activity to reduce the number of options to two in each case.	
35	Mixed doubles		**Mixed doubles** consolidates the children's spelling skills, drawing on knowledge of word structure and spelling patterns, including the use of double letters. It reinforces understanding and application of the **-ed** suffix for the past tense. It focuses on verbs that end with a consonant following the phonemes **/a/, /e/, /i/, /o/** or **/u/**. The final consonant is doubled before the **-ed** suffix is added, in order to retain the short vowel sound. Note that after long vowel phonemes the final consonant is not doubled: for example, *cheat, groan, shout, greet, turn*, but **r** is doubled when it is the final consonant and part of the phonemes **/ar/, /er/, /ir/, /ur/**: for example, *purred, starred, stirred*. Use the example, *hop*, to show the children why the consonant is doubled (adding **-ed** without doubling the consonant produces *hoped*, changing the **/o/** phoneme to **/oa/**). During the plenary session the children could read the past tense verbs aloud and compare these with words made by adding **-ed** without doubling the final consonant. Other useful verbs include *beg, chug, clip, dip, drag, drip, flap, flop, hum, mop, nag, nip, nod, plan, prod, rub, scrap, skim, skip, slop, strip, trim*. You could also ask the children to read aloud verbs formed by adding **-ed** to words ending in **g**, with and without doubling the **g**: for example, *wag (wagged), waged*. Point out that in the past tense of *wag* the **/g/** phoneme changes to **/j/** if the **g** is not doubled.	
36	Match and sort: -ed		**Match and sort: -ed** helps the children to learn to spell, drawing on knowledge of word structure, and reinforces understanding and application of the **-ed** suffix for the past tense. They learn to categorise words according to their spelling pattern. The cut-out cards can be used in different ways: ask the children (working individually or in pairs) to match each base word to its past tense and then sort them into sets according to what happens to the base word when the **-ed** ending is added, or give each child a base word or a past tense and ask them to find their partners and then get into groups according to what happens to the base word when the **-ed** ending is added. You could let them decide how to sort the cards or remind them about base words that do not change when **-ed** is added, those that lose the final **e**, those ending in **y** that changes to **i** and those ending in a consonant that is doubled. These rules become 'second nature' when the children are exposed to them thoroughly through reading, so listing or displaying the words and constructing sentences from them that the children then read back are also important elements in this process. Use the CD-ROM to adjust the selection of words so that you can repeat this activity using different examples.	
37	Sad to say	**7. Understanding and interpreting texts** Draw together ideas and information from across a whole text, using simple signposts in the text	**Sad to say** helps the children to consider story structure, identify the main and other characters and consider how they affect one another's feelings and the events of the story. Also encourage them to give reasons why events happen and, where applicable, what makes characters change in a story they have read or listened to. Suitable stories include: *See you at the Match* by Margaret Joy (Faber & Faber) (or the extract entitled *The Autograph* in *The Kingfisher Treasury of Stories for Seven Year Olds*), about a boy who breaks his leg and cannot go to the football match; and *Jessy and the Bridesmaid's Dress* by Rachel Anderson & Shelagh McNicholas (Young Lions *Jets* series, HarperCollins), about a girl with Downs' Syndrome who wants to be a bridesmaid and is sad because her teacher is leaving the school when she gets married.	**Reading AF2** Understand, describe, select or retrieve information, events or ideas from texts and use quotation and reference to text **Reading AF3** Deduce, infer or interpret information, events or ideas from texts **Reading AF1** Use a range of strategies including accurate decoding of text, to read for meaning **Reading AF4** Identify and comment on the structure and organisation of texts, including grammatical and presentational features at text level **Reading AF5** Explain and comment on writers' uses of language, including grammatical and literary features at word and sentence level
38	Amazing Grace	**7. Understanding and interpreting texts** Give some reasons for why things happen or characters change	**Amazing Grace** is based on *Amazing Grace* by Mary Hoffman (Frances Lincoln) and is set in a familiar environment (school). It focuses on the feelings, personality and talents of the main character, Grace. You could stop at various points in the story and ask how Grace feels and what she might do. Ask which characters helped her. This could be linked with work in citizenship on Taking part and Living in a diverse world. Issues of racism and equal opportunities could be discussed at a simple level (Can a girl play the part of Peter Pan? Is there any reason why Grace, who is black, cannot play this part?). The children could look for examples to show why Grace would be good in this role (she is good at acting and will work hard at it).	**Reading AF2** Understand, describe, select or retrieve information, events or ideas from texts and use quotation and reference to text **Reading AF3** Deduce, infer or interpret information, events or ideas from texts **Reading AF1** Use a range of strategies including accurate decoding of text, to read for meaning **Reading AF4** Identify and comment on the structure and organisation of texts, including grammatical and presentational features at text level **Reading AF5** Explain and comment on writers' uses of language, including grammatical and literary features at word and sentence level
39	Leon and Bob story map		**Leon and Bob story map** encourages the children to engage with books through exploring interpretations and to explain their reactions to texts. It also develops skills in identifying the main events of a story and retelling them in the correct order. As with the previous activities you could also draw out how the main character felt at different points in the story and how his imaginary friend Bob and real friend Bob helped.	
40	Feelings		**Feelings** helps the children to notice words in the text which tell them how a character is feeling. You could base this on characters in the same story or different stories by the same author. Point out the verbs used instead of *said* and ask the children what they tell the reader about the character's feelings. Discuss which of the feelings could be used to describe more than one person: for example, *excited* could be used for Runa and Sam. The children could then look for similar examples in other books and highlight them in photocopies of the texts on the interactive whiteboard or record them in a table. Encourage them to use these words in their own writing. This activity provides opportunities for children to read sentences aloud, using appropriate expression.	

Title	Objective	Activity	Writing AFs	Page
Salim's new bike	**9. Creating and shaping texts** Sustain form in narrative, including use of person and time	**Salim's new bike** develops skills in sustaining form in narrative and using appropriate language to make sections hang together. It provides a familiar setting and an opening for a story that the children can develop. They should notice a clue in the opening as to what might happen next: Salim takes care to lock up his bike and he is looking forward to going to the park with his dad to ride it the next day – so something might happen to prevent this, for example, his bike is damaged or stolen. You could first help the children to write notes about this as they did in **A special treat** (pages 51–53). Discuss whether it is better to say exactly what happened at this point or to leave the reader wondering who harmed or stole the bike but to give a clue. The children can then write their notes, as a class or individually.	**All Writing AFs, especially:** **Writing AF1** Write imaginative, interesting and thoughtful texts **Writing AF2** Produce texts which are appropriate to task, reader and purpose **Writing AF7** Select appropriate and effective vocabulary	41
The competition	**10. Text structure and organisation** Use planning to establish clear sections for writing	**The competition** provides a scaffold to help the children to use planning to establish clear sections for writing in a familiar setting. You could begin by showing them advertising features or forms for competitions for children and asking them to imagine someone reading the information and entering the competition. What would he or she do? Model how to make notes: for example, if they say *Ellie read the heading Win a Mountain Bike. She saw that she had to paint a picture of someone riding a bike* you could say 'I'll write that down, but it doesn't need to be a sentence because we're just making notes,' and write *Ellie reads win mountain bike. Paint pic of someone on bike.* You could continue in this way for each section of the planning, perhaps with the page displayed on an interactive whiteboard. Ask the children to talk about the main character preparing the competition entry. Then ask what might go wrong, either before or after it is posted: for example, the dog chews it, a baby brother or sister daubs paint on it, it is thrown out by mistake with the rubbish, it is sent to the wrong address, she forgets to put her name and address on it and realises this after she has posted it. The children can then suggest ideas for solving the problem. Other characters might help.	**Writing AF3** Organise and present whole texts effectively, sequencing and structuring information, ideas and events **Writing AF4** Construct paragraphs and use cohesion within and between paragraphs	42
A special treat: 1, 2 and 3		**A special treat: 1, 2** and **3** provide a story structure to help the children to write their story in six sections, which could be arranged as six chapters. The starting points help them to sustain form in narrative and to use appropriate language to help sections hang together. These pages are intended to be used over a series of writing sessions to encourage the children to spend time on the structure and details of the story: opening (introducing the main character); the main event (he gets tickets for a football match); his reaction (excitement, showing off to friends); something happens (he is going to miss the match because of this); events happen to sort this out; ending (including a surprise and an indication to the reader about what might happen next or how the story has affected Simon: for example, it might stop him showing off). You could link this with work in citizenship on relationships: sharing a friend's good news, jealousy, how to keep friends, showing off and its effects on friends.		43–45
Chosen		**Chosen** helps the children to plan a story about a character who is chosen for something special. Ask them for their ideas about what this could be for or for their own memories of being chosen for something. They could work on this individually, with a partner (asking one another the questions and coming up with answers) or it could be used to support a group or whole-class hot-seating activity. Alternatively, let the children explore the story through role-play. Make a note of the questions and answers (perhaps on an interactive whiteboard) and help the children to develop them into a story.		46
Cross the road	**11. Sentence structure and punctuation** Write simple and compound sentences and begin to use subordination in relation to time and reason	**Cross the road** helps the children to write simple sentences saying who did the action, what they did, and where. Those who undertake the extension activity could add a word or two to say when the action took place: for example, yesterday, this morning, this afternoon, last night, on Monday. Encourage each pair of children to share their completed page with another pair and to read one another's sentences aloud.	**Writing AF5** Vary sentences for clarity, purpose and effect **Writing AF6** Write with technical accuracy of syntax and punctuation in phrases, clauses and sentences	47
Sentence wall		**Sentence wall** develops skills in building longer sentences involving place and time. The children begin with a character and time. They add words or phrases to say where or when the action took place. Encourage them to read the sentences aloud to check that they make sense. They could share their completed page with another pair of children who could check that they are sentences.		48
Where words		**Where words** is about prepositions, although this term is not yet introduced to the children. These words help the children to compose compound sentences with subordination involving place. Remind them of the questions they have been asked when building sentences in their previous work: Who (or what) did the action? What did they do? Where? When? and Why? The children could mime actions involving location or direction and the others could identify the Where words and then compose sentences to say what they are doing: for example, *Kit is crawling along the mat, Mair is hopping across the floor.*		49
Past change	**11. Sentence structure and punctuation** Compose sentences using tense consistently (present and past)	**Past change** introduces the past and present tenses. You could begin by demonstrating an action and asking the children what you are doing. Write up their responses as sentences in the second and first person: for example, *You are writing, I am writing, You are reading, I am reading.* Tell them about doing the same actions in the past: for example, *Yesterday I was writing, Yesterday I was reading.* Write these up and ask the children which words have changed. Introduce the shorter forms of these tenses: *I drive to school/I drove to school, You walk to school/You walked to school.* You could link this with word-level work on the ways in which words change according to meaning.	**Writing AF5** Vary sentences for clarity, purpose and effect **Writing AF6** Write with technical accuracy of syntax and punctuation in phrases, clauses and sentences	50

Year 2 Narrative unit 2 Traditional stories

Activity name	Strand and learning objectives	Notes on the activities	Assessment Focus	Page number
Story mix	**1. Speaking** Tell real and imagined stories using the conventions of familiar story language	**Story mix** is about telling stories using the conventions of familiar story language. The children begin with characters from the well-known stories *Snow White and the Seven Dwarfs* and *Jack and the Beanstalk* and are asked to think about how they might respond to one another and what they might say and do. They could read the original stories for themselves or listen to them on a tape or being read by an adult or another child before re-telling one of them with the introduction of the new character. Ask them about the problems the characters face and how they might help one another to solve them. Link this with work in creating and shaping texts (drawing on knowledge of texts). **Vocabulary:** *character, evil, fairytale, good, problem, re-tell, setting, solve, tale, story, traditional.*	**Speaking and listening AF1** Talk in purposeful and imaginative ways to explore ideas and feelings, adapting and varying structure and vocabulary according to purpose, listeners, and content	51
Story listener The best dishcloth: 1 and 2	**2. Listening and responding** Respond to presentations by describing characters, repeating some highlights and commenting constructively	**Story listener** focuses on responding by commenting constructively. The story could be read by another child or it could be on a professionally recorded video or DVD. Encourage the children to comment in their responses: for example, explain why they could not hear the story well, at what points in the story the reader looked at the audience, and how this helped, what the reader did when using his or her face or actions or how the reader's voice changed from one character to another and how well he or she kept the same voice for the same character. **Vocabulary:** *actions, audience, expression, change, story, voice.* **The best dishcloth: 1** and **2** involve responding to a presentation by asking questions and commenting constructively. It can be used in connection with work in science on testing dishcloths for absorbency; the children could convert it to instructions for carrying out the test. If some children are listening to others who are reading, the chart could be displayed on the interactive whiteboard to help them to comment on the results and to answer the 'true or false' questions on page 62. **Vocabulary:** *absorbent, audience, dishcloth, fair test, false, J-cloth, speaker, towelling, true.*	**Speaking and listening AF2** Listen and respond to others, including in pairs and groups, shaping meanings through suggestions, comments, and question	52 53–54
Rama and Sita: 1 and 2	**4. Drama** Present part of traditional stories, own stories or work from different parts of the curriculum for members of their own class	**Rama and Sita: 1** and **2** This story could be read as a shared text in connection with RE and with text-level work on traditional stories. **Vocabulary:** *character, determination, evil, excitement, expression, fear, feeling, puppet, role, story, voice.*	**Speaking and listening AF3** Create and sustain different roles and scenarios, adapting techniques in a range of dramatic activities to explore texts, ideas, and issues	55–56
Name clapping Happy families: 1 and 2	**5. Word recognition: decoding (reading) and encoding (spelling)** Read and spell less common alternative graphemes including trigraphs	**Name clapping** focuses on a routine to help the children to read longer words. They listen to a word and learn to separate it into syllables. Begin by choosing the name of a child in the class that has one syllable. Repeat this for other names with two, three or four syllables. You could also display pictures of footballers, say and clap their family names as football chants: *Beck-ham, Crouch, Fer-din-and, Ger-rard, Ny-a-tang-ga, Ow-en, Ron-al-do, Roo-ney.* The children could then clap the syllables of a name from a list (for example, story characters) and the others guess who it is. **Happy families: 1** and **2** help the children to read less common alternative graphemes, including trigraphs. They use analogy to group words according to their spelling patterns. For a less challenging activity use each page separately. As an extension activity they could use analogy to help them to spell words they hear (a recording of words could be prepared before the lesson): *blotch, butcher, catch, crutch, hatch, hutch, itch, latch, match, stitch, thatch, watch, witch; haughty, slaughter; calm; worse, worth.*	**Reading AF1** Use a range of strategies including accurate decoding of text, to read for meaning **Writing AF8** Use correct spelling	57 58–59
Long words: 1 and 2	**5. Word recognition: decoding (reading) and encoding (spelling)** Read high and medium frequency words independently and automatically	**Long words: 1** and **2** focus on a routine to help the children to spell longer words, some with less common alternative graphemes. They listen to a word and learn to separate it into syllables, after which they draw a phoneme frame on which to write the phonemes for each syllable. They should have had the chance to manipulate word tiles or use a wipe-off board before attempting to draw the phoneme boxes. Demonstrate the routine by saying and clapping a two-syllable word (for example, *pencil, ruler* or *carpet*). On the whiteboard, draw a box for each syllable and point to the syllable as you clap and say the word. Ask the children to write the letters for the first syllable and show them. Discuss any differences and show which is correct. Repeat this for the second syllable. Do this with another word but ask the children to draw a box for each syllable. Say and clap the word and ask them to write the letters for the first syllable. Repeat this for the second syllable. Do the same for another word, but this time ask the children to draw lines in the boxes to separate the phonemes. Summarise the routine: clap, count, draw, write. Ask them to use this routine to help them to complete these pages.	**Reading AF1** Use a range of strategies including accurate decoding of text, to read for meaning **Writing AF8** Use correct spelling	60–61
In short	**6. Word structure and spelling** Spell with increasing accuracy and confidence, drawing on word recognition and knowledge of word structure, and spelling patterns including common inflections and use of double letters	**In short** develops skills in spelling with increasing accuracy and confidence, drawing on knowledge of word structure. It focuses on the structure of contractions. The children will probably be able to read these words long before they understand how they are formed. They learn that the position of the apostrophe indicates a missing letter or letters. It will be helpful to use interactive whiteboard tools or individual wipe-off boards so that the children can physically change a word to its contracted form.	**Writing AF8** Use correct spelling	62
Syllables and phonemes: 1 and 2	**6. Word structure and spelling** Read and spell less common alternative graphemes including trigraphs	**Syllables and phonemes: 1** and **2** help the children to read longer words, some with less common alternative graphemes, by sounding and blending the phonemes in each syllable, then joining the syllables and saying the words.	**Writing AF8** Use correct spelling	63–64

Page	Activity	Objective	Notes	Assessment focuses
65	What if…?	**7. Understanding and interpreting texts** — Draw together ideas and information from across a whole text, using simple signposts in the text	**What if…?** provides an opportunity to consider an alternative version of the fairytale *The Sleeping Beauty* by changing the main character to a boy. Ask the children if the good fairies would give the same 'gifts' and what bad 'gift' the wicked fairy might give. How would these change the story? Also discuss how the title of the story might be changed.	**Reading AF2** Understand, describe, select or retrieve information, events or ideas from texts and use quotation and reference to text **Reading AF3** Deduce, infer or interpret information, events or ideas from texts **Reading AF1** Use a range of strategies including accurate decoding of text, to read for meaning **Reading AF4** Identify and comment on the structure and organisation of texts, including grammatical and presentational features at text level **Reading AF5** Explain and comment on writers' uses of language, including grammatical and literary features at word and sentence level
66	Character change	**9. Creating and shaping texts** — Draw on knowledge and experience of texts in deciding and planning what and how to write	**Character change** encourages the children to draw on knowledge and experience of traditional stories in planning how to write. It helps them to consider the ways in which characters are presented in stories in order to use these techniques in their own writing. They learn to express ideas about a character using evidence from the text to justify their opinion. Here they compare *Little Red Riding Hood* in the traditional tale with *Little Red Riding Hood* in *The True Story of Little Red Riding Hood* (see www.standards.dfes.gov.uk/primaryframeworks/literacy/planning/Year2/Narrativestories/unit2/resources). If they want to, children could make up some qualities for a different Red Riding Hood in a different story.	**All Writing AFs, especially:** **Writing AF1** Write imaginative, interesting and thoughtful texts **Writing AF2** Produce texts which are appropriate to task, reader and purpose **Writing AF7** Select appropriate and effective vocabulary
67	Good wolf and bad wolf on screen	**9. Creating and shaping texts** — Select from different presentational features to suit particular writing purposes on paper and on screen	**Good Wolf and Bad Wolf on screen** helps the children to draw on knowledge and experience of texts in deciding and planning what to write and to select from different presentational features to suit their writing. They consider how characters are presented on screen to bring out their personal characteristics and develop an understanding of how words, images and sounds can communicate information about characters. Here the focus is on the effect created by the background. It is also useful if they have a selection of music and other sound recordings to listen to and from which they can choose the most suitable for creating the impression of the good and bad wolves.	
68–71	The three bully goats Gruff The bullied troll The Troll's diary The Troll's solution	**10. Text structure and organisation** — Use planning to establish clear sections for writing	**The Three Bully Goats Gruff, The bullied troll, The Troll's diary** and **The Troll's solution** provide a structure to help the children to use planning to establish clear sections for writing their own version of the traditional tale *The Three Billy Goats Gruff*. They draw on knowledge and experience of texts as they consider the story from the point of view of the troll, who is harassed by the family of 'bully' goats. At this stage they are not telling the story in detail; they are planning the outline. These pages can provide a useful setting for examining the problem of bullying at school and what the children should do if they are bullied or know of anyone else who is a victim. They also introduce or revisit letter writing (page 77). You could point out that letter writers should put their address at the top of the page (indicate the top right) and the date, but that on this page they are concentrating on what to say in the letter. Help them to make notes during lessons on citizenship about what can be done to help someone who is being bullied and then use these to help them to write their letters to the troll. Encourage them to express sympathy with the troll: for example, *I am sorry that you are being bullied. I'd like to help you*. During another lesson they could copy the text onto a letter format that includes their address and the date. You could even set up a 'mailbox' for the troll (and make a model of him and a large picture of the bridge) and write replies to the children's letters. Another text format included here is **The Troll's diary** (page 78). They should write this as if they are the troll. Encourage them to consider the bridge crossing and to say what else the goats might do. Again, link it with a citizenship lesson in which the children list the actions that can be classed as bullying and how the victim should respond. They can use this list to help them to fill in the troll's diary, noting who did the bullying (which one of the bully goats, or perhaps another animal co-opted into their gang). **The Troll's solution** (page 79) helps the children to follow the story structure after the letter and diary have been used to write about the problem. Model how to write in the past tense and the third person (these terms will not be used but point out the difference between story language and the language of the troll's diary). This, too, can be linked with work in citizenship in which they learn how the problem of bullying can be solved in various ways, depending on the situation, and involving the help of other people. They introduce characters who can help the troll and make notes about how they help to solve the problem. The last part of the story structure – the ending – can then be written. Here, encourage the children to think up more creative endings than 'The troll lived happily ever after.' They could, for example, write about how the bully goats mended their ways (or were made to) or about new friendships between the troll, the reformed bully goats and other characters. You could choose to work from only three out of four of the pages if that seems appropriate for the class.	**Writing AF3** Organise and present whole texts effectively, sequencing and structuring information, ideas and events **Writing AF4** Construct paragraphs and use cohesion within and between paragraphs
72 73	Sentence maker Link up	**11. Sentence structure and punctuation** — Write simple and compound sentences and begin to use subordination in relation to time and reason	**Sentence maker** develops skills in writing simple sentences without the support of a ready-planned format. The children are required to make a note of the words their counters land on and arrange these to form sentences, if they can. Some children might need adult help in order to recognise when they have collected enough words to make a sentence. You could ask them if they have a word for *who did the action* and a word for *what they did*. Then ask them if they need anything else: for example, words for *where they did the action*. **Link up** provides sections of sentences saying who did the action, what they did and when. From these, the children create longer sentences. You could also play a game in which the class is split into three groups. Allocate to each group: the *Who?* group should write the name of a person or animal: for example, *Our teacher* (or the teacher's name); *My mum* or *I*. The *What did they do?* group should write an action: for example, *climbed a tree, whistled a tune, sang a song, beat a drum*. The *When?* group should write a word or group of words which say when the action happened: for example, *before breakfast, this morning, on Friday*. Invite a child from each group to come out and hold up his or her card, beginning with the *Who?* group, followed by *What did they do?* and then *When?* Invite a volunteer to read these aloud in the correct order. Draw out that this is a sentence.	**Writing AF5** Vary sentences for clarity, purpose and effect **Writing AF6** Write with technical accuracy of syntax and punctuation in phrases, clauses and sentences

Year 2 Narrative unit 3 Different stories by the same author

Activity name	Strand and learning objectives	Notes on the activities	Assessment Focus	Page number
Surprising endings: 1 and 2 My surprising ending	**2. Listening and responding** Listen to others in class, ask relevant questions and follow instructions	**Surprising endings: 1 and 2 and My surprising ending** encourage the children to listen to others and remember key points. Their responses require them to describe characters, repeat some highlights and comment constructively before telling their own stories based on what they have listened to. These activities are also useful for developing the children's writing skills (Creating and shaping texts). **Vocabulary:** *beginning, character, ending, event, main character, problem, surprise.*	**Speaking and listening AF2** Listen and respond to others, including in pairs and groups, shaping meanings through suggestions, comments, and question	74–76
Charity choice: 1 and 2 Fundraisers Fundraising plan	**3. Group discussion and interaction** Work effectively in groups by ensuring that each group member takes a turn challenging, supporting and moving on	**Charity choice: 1 and 2, Fundraisers** and **Fundraising plan** encourage the children to work effectively in groups by ensuring that everyone contributes and takes turns to speak, challenge or move on. **Fundraisers** and **Fundraising plan** provides support in considering alternatives, reaching agreement, agreeing the next steps to take, allocating tasks and recognising each member's contribution. They can be used in sequence in connection with work in citizenship on Taking part. To prepare for these activities you could invite speakers from charities to present talks to the children; also provide leaflets and information from charities' websites. Invite the children to talk about their experiences of fundraising events such as jumble sales, sponsored events, raffles and quizzes and to identify the pros and cons of each. **Fundraisers** could be modified using the CD-ROM to feature a different set of options for the children to discuss, and **Fundraising plan** could be used to help in preparing for a real charity fundraising event. During the plenary sessions after these activities, encourage children to reflect briefly on how their group discussions went. Did everyone contribute/agree? **Vocabulary:** *charity, choose, collect, decide, funds, fundraising, plan, support, vote.*	**Speaking and listening AF2** Listen and respond to others, including in pairs and groups, shaping meanings through suggestions, comments, and question	77–80
Moving day	**4. Drama** Adopt appropriate roles in small or large groups and consider alternative courses of action	**Moving day.** Ideas to discuss include what to say to make people feel welcome and how to communicate with others in a new situation. **Vocabulary:** *act, enact, make friends, move, problem, removal, role, solve, story.*	**Speaking and listening AF3** Create and sustain different roles and scenarios, adapting techniques to explore texts, ideas, and issues	81
Mind-readers: 1 and 2	**5. Word recognition: decoding (reading) and encoding (spelling)** Read independently and with increasing fluency longer and less familiar texts **5. Word recognition: decoding (reading) and encoding (spelling)** Read and spell less common alternative graphemes including trigraphs	**Mind-readers: 1 and 2** promote independent reading and spelling with increasing accuracy, drawing on word recognition and knowledge of word structure and less common alternative graphemes. They can be used to help the children to learn high-frequency and topic words by developing their ability to identify the potentially difficult element/s in a word: for example, the **gn** grapheme for /n/ and the **ea** grapheme for /e/. The children could begin by clapping the syllables of the words in the word-bank and writing the numbers of syllables beside the words. They could also draw the phoneme frames for these words on scrap paper or create them on the interactive whiteboard, and then match them to those provided with the word descriptions.	**Reading AF1** Use a range of strategies including accurate decoding of text, to read for meaning **Writing AF8** Use correct spelling	82–83
What are you doing?	**6. Word structure and spelling** Spell with increasing accuracy and confidence, drawing on word recognition and knowledge of word structure, and spelling patterns including common inflections and use of double letters	**What are you doing?** helps the children to spell with increasing accuracy and confidence, drawing on word recognition and knowledge of word structure and spelling patterns. It also provides practice in reading and spelling high-frequency words independently and automatically. You could introduce the term *suffix* for an affix attached to the end of a word (a group of letters that are added to the end of a word to change the word and make it a different type of word). In this activity the suffix -**ing** does not affect the spelling of the base word. You could demonstrate why the base words need to be changed by asking the children what is wrong with the following: *I am go to school, I am eat a cake, I am watch television, I am look for my pen.* Ask them to correct the sentences and to say which word they changed and how they changed it.	**Writing AF8** Use correct spelling	84
Let's ask Rapunzel	**8. Engaging with and responding to texts** Engage with books through exploring and enacting interpretations	**Let's ask Rapunzel** provides support for a 'hot-seating' activity in which children take the 'hot-seat' as Rapunzel and the others ask them questions. You could encourage them to explore why the witch kept Rapunzel in a tower, what and how Rapunzel learned (she didn't go to school), the songs she sang, what she wore, what she could see from the window in the tower and so on. The children will be able to answer some of the questions using what they know from the story. For other questions, they will have to use what they know about the characters in the story to make their answers seem possible. This sheet can serve as a model for the children's own sheets about other characters.	**All Reading AFs, especially:** **Reading AF6** Identify and comment on writers' purposes and viewpoints and the overall effect of the text on the reader **Reading AF3** Deduce, infer or interpret information, events or ideas from texts **Reading AF7** Relate texts to their social, cultural and historical contexts and literary traditions	85

Year 2 Narrative unit 4 Extended stories / Significant authors

Character quest Reasons	**7. Understanding and interpreting texts** Give some reasons for why things happen or characters change	**Character quest** helps the children to focus on aspects of a character created by an author about whom they are learning. You could copy this page and display it on an interactive whiteboard; invite the children to add information in text boxes or on 'stickies'. Encourage the others to question this information; they could ask 'How do you know?' and those who wrote it could supply evidence from the story. Also discuss what they are not told in the story but can guess or imagine – and ask for evidence to support these guesses. Ask the children to think about whether the character changes during the story and, if so, in what ways. This kind of format can help with the children's own writing and creation of characters. **Reasons** focuses on identifying and explaining events in a story by a significant children's author: *A Necklace of Raindrops* by Joan Aiken (Puffin). It can be linked with work on questions. The children are required to think about the characters and events in the story and to say why they happened. It is useful to draw out common story themes, such as characters repaying help and kindness in the past when those who helped them face problems, and seemingly powerless characters, such as a fish, a bird and a mouse, having the power to overcome evil and affect the course of events.	**Reading AF2** Understand, describe, select or retrieve information, events or ideas from texts and use quotation and reference to text **Reading AF3** Deduce, infer or interpret information, events or ideas from texts **Reading AF1** Use a range of strategies including accurate decoding of text, to read for meaning **Reading AF4** Identify and comment on the structure and organisation of texts, including grammatical and presentational features at text level **Reading AF5** Explain and comment on writers' uses of language, including grammatical and literary features at word and sentence level	96 97
Character clues	**8. Engaging with and responding to texts** Engage with books through exploring and enacting interpretations	**Character clues** develops the children's skills in deducing what characters are like from descriptions and from recounts of their actions. Help them to use details in the passage to form an opinion of a character. At a simple level, they could decide whether the character is good or bad and then say what is good and what is bad about him or her. Ask them to use at least one word from the word-bank to describe each character.	**All Reading AFs, especially:** **Reading AF6** Identify and comment on writers' purposes and viewpoints and the overall effect of the text on the reader **Reading AF3** Deduce, infer or interpret information, events or ideas from texts **Reading AF7** Relate texts to their social, cultural and historical contexts and literary traditions	98
Story settings Story character The wish The wish dialogue The wish consequences	**9. Creating and shaping texts** Sustain form in narrative, including use of person and time	**Story settings** encourages the children to draw on their knowledge and experience of texts in deciding and planning what to write. It provides a selection of story settings in which they can set an extended story. They could cut out the cards and choose one, then talk about what might happen there. The picture could be glued into a notebook in which the children could write notes about the setting and the kind of story that might happen there. They could talk about the setting in groups and, with some guidance, suggest the kinds of events that might take place there before they cut out the setting of their choice. Ask them to imagine stepping into the setting. What might they see and hear? What would it feel like? Who might be there? What kind of thing might happen? **Story character** encourages the children to draw on their knowledge and experience of texts in deciding and planning what to write. It focuses on a story character. They are invited to imagine their story character and make notes to help them to introduce him or her. Encourage them to think about the character's lifestyle in the chosen setting and what might happen there. The story plans from previous sections could then be used to help in planning the story. **The wish, The wish dialogue** and **The wish consequences** develops skills in sustaining form in narrative. It provides a format for planning an extended story that features a wish, a planning sheet (with hints) for writing dialogue based on these notes and a format for planning the rest of the story. It is useful if they have first read other stories in which wishes are granted and discussed whether the wishes were wise choices and what happened because of them. Having made notes about the wish, the children write the dialogue for the scene in which the wish was granted (page 102), they then consider the consequences and problems and make notes about these and the solution. These pages can then be used to help the children to key in or write an extended story using the structure provided and incorporating the dialogue they wrote. As an extension children could write the ending of the story when they have completed page 103.	**All Writing AFs, especially:** **Writing AF1** Write imaginative, interesting and thoughtful texts **Writing AF2** Produce texts which are appropriate to task, reader and purpose **Writing AF7** Select appropriate and effective vocabulary	99 100 101–103
Past mistakes Put it right	**11. Sentence structure and punctuation** Compose sentences using tense consistently (present and past)	**Past mistakes** focuses on the correct forms and spellings of the past tense, including those of irregular verbs such as to say, eat. This can be linked with word-level work on spelling and suffixes. Draw out that most past tenses end with **-ed** and ask the children to spot any which do not. You could create a class wall chart/word-bank of 'normal' past tenses to which the children can contribute. Also challenge them to find exceptions and to write them on to a wall chart of exceptions. Useful verbs to include are: run/ran, choose/chose, find/found, come/came, make/made, see/saw, hear/heard, feel/felt, bring/brought, send/sent, teach/taught, read/read, slide/slid, hide/hid, draw/drew, drink/drank, swim/swam, fling/flung, catch/caught, say/said, ring/rang, fly/flew, grow/grew, throw/threw, know/knew, and blow/blew. **Put it right** develops skills in using tenses consistently. Remind the children of their previous work on tenses and tell them that you are going to read out a passage which has mistakes in it where the wrong tense is used. Ask them to listen carefully and to put up their hand when they hear a mistake. Draw out that the day at the zoo happened in the past and so the words for actions should show this. You could introduce the terms verb and tense if appropriate.	**Writing AF5** Vary sentences for clarity, purpose and effect **Writing AF6** Write with technical accuracy of syntax and punctuation in phrases, clauses and sentences	104 105

Year 2 Non-Fiction unit 1 Instructions

Activity name	Strand and learning objectives	Notes on the activities	Assessment Focus	Page number
Caterpillar talk How well did you speak? A famous person	**1. Speaking** Speak with clarity and use appropriate intonation when reading and reciting texts	**Caterpillar talk** is about using intonation when speaking or reading. You could begin by showing a video clip of a tense moment from a film but with the sound turned off. Ask the children how the people feel and how they can tell. Ask them to imagine the same scene on the radio. What might they hear? Encourage them to express the characters' feelings. They can then try 'caterpillar talk'. They could also say *Caterpillar* to sound scary, excited or sad. Link this with reciting poetry in literacy lessons. **Vocabulary:** *angry, bad-tempered, cheerful, excited, expression, jolly, lively, sleepy, sound, tone of voice.* **How well did you speak?** encourages the children to speak with clarity, using appropriate intonation. It could be used in conjunction with any activity to focus the children's attention on clear speaking, looking at the audience and using expression. Also use it to help the children to assess their own progress. **Vocabulary:** *clearly, expression, speak, spoke, voice.* **A famous person** supports the children in planning a talk and gives them a chance to practise speaking clearly using appropriate intonation to add interest when they tell an audience about the well-known person they have found out about. You could give them a free choice or let them choose from a list of people about whom you have collected information sources. As they plan their talk, encourage them to practise using different tones of voice to express excitement, interest or surprise or when talking about something sad. **Vocabulary:** *birthplace, date of birth, events, family name, famous, important, personal name.*	**Speaking and listening AF1** Talk in purposeful and imaginative ways to explore ideas and feelings, adapting and varying structure and vocabulary according to purpose, listeners, and content	106 107 108
A day out	**2. Listening and responding** Listen to others in class, ask relevant questions and follow instructions	**A day out** focuses on listening to others in the class, asking relevant questions and remembering some specific points. This page is designed to be used in a 'jigsawing' activity in which the children listen to a friend talking about a day out. They then tell another group about their friend's day out. Some children might be able to think up other questions of their own. It could also be used in conjunction with listening to a talk by an adult so that they can tell children in another class about it. **Vocabulary:** *answer, listen, outing, question, speak, talk, tell.*	**Speaking and listening AF2** Listen and respond to others, including in pairs and groups, shaping meanings through suggestions, comments, and question	109
A class pet	**3. Group discussion and interaction** Ensure everyone contributes, allocate tasks, and consider alternatives and reach agreement	**A class pet** presents an opportunity for the children to participate in a group discussion to which everyone contributes and which involves allocating tasks, considering alternatives and reaching an agreement as they find out about an animal and discuss its appropriateness for a class pet. They will need help in finding information about the animal from information texts such as books, leaflets and websites such as the RSPCA (www.rspca.org.uk), PDSA (www.pdsa.org.uk), Dogs Trust (www.dogstrust.org.uk) and Cat Protection (www.cats.org.uk). Ask them to think about whether the animal would be safe and happy at school and whether the school would be able to look after it properly. To encourage the children to participate fully in the discussion, ask them to listen to each speaker and if he or she does not tell them about feeding, bedding, exercise and the type of home the animal needs, they should ask. You could also point out that perhaps no animal would be suitable. This could be combined with work in citizenship on Animals and us and the children could also discuss what kinds of pets are suitable for which people (people with different lifestyles and homes). **Vocabulary:** *agreement, animal, care, decide, discuss, feeding, happiness, health, listen, opinion, pet, question, view.*	**Speaking and listening AF2** Listen and respond to others, including in pairs and groups, shaping meanings through suggestions, comments, and question	110
Picture clues	**5. Word recognition:** decoding (reading) and encoding (spelling) Read and spell less common alternative graphemes including trigraphs	**Picture clues** helps the children to read and spell words containing less common alternative graphemes through introducing strategies to help: the use of mnemonics (both visual and verbal). Other words for which mnemonics might be useful include *build, buy, cupboard*. The children could suggest their own sentences or pictures to help them to remember the 'tricky bits' of the words. They should discuss other words they find difficult and work together on memory aids for them. Mnemonics are personal, as everyone remembers things in different ways according to their own learning style: visual, verbal and so on.	**Reading AF1** Use a range of strategies including accurate decoding of text, to read for meaning **Writing AF8** Use correct spelling	111
Base words with -ful	**6. Word structure and spelling** Spell with increasing accuracy and confidence, drawing on word recognition and knowledge of word structure, and spelling patterns including common inflections and use of double letters	**Base words with -ful** is about spelling with increasing accuracy and confidence, drawing on word recognition and knowledge of word structure and spelling patterns, including common inflections. Note that few base words change when **-ful** is added: most of those that change end in **ll** or **y:** for example, *skill/skilful, duty/dutiful, fancy/fanciful, bounty/bountiful and beauty/beautiful.*	**Writing AF8** Use correct spelling	112
Hide and seek Ladybird program	**7. Understanding and interpreting texts** Draw together ideas and information from across a whole text, using simple signposts in the text	**Hide and seek** develops skills in reading and following instructions. The children find where the gnomes are hiding in the picture. They could talk in their groups about how good the instructions were. Give them the solutions and ask them if they found these places. You could link this with work on word reading strategies (silent *g*). **Ladybird program** is about reading and following precise instructions. It links with work in ICT on programmable toys. The children could also work in pairs with one acting as instructor and the other acting as the robot that follows the instructions. Ask the children to notice the first word of each instruction (Go) and compare this with other instructions they have read. They could compile a list of instruction words: for example, *sit, turn, wait, stop.* Copy the grid onto card and provide ladybird cut-outs for children to move according to the instructions.	**Reading AF2** Understand, describe, select or retrieve information, events or ideas from texts and use quotation and reference to text **Reading AF3** Deduce, infer or interpret information, events or ideas from texts **Reading AF1** Use a range of strategies including accurate decoding of text, to read for meaning **Reading AF4** Identify and comment on the structure and organisation of texts, including grammatical and presentational features at text level **Reading AF5** Explain and comment on writers' uses of language, including grammatical and literary features at word and sentence level	113 114

Unit	Objective	Assessment focuses	Description	Page
Stripy lolly	**7. Understanding and interpreting texts** Explain organisational features of texts, including alphabetical order, layout, diagrams, captions, hyperlinks and bullet points	**Reading AF2** Understand, describe, select or retrieve information, events or ideas from texts and use quotation and reference to text **Reading AF3** Deduce, infer or interpret information, events or ideas from texts **Reading AF1** Use a range of strategies including accurate decoding of text, to read for meaning **Reading AF4** Identify and comment on the structure and organisation of texts, including grammatical and presentational features at text level **Reading AF5** Explain and comment on writers' uses of language, including grammatical and literary features at word and sentence level	Stripy lolly provides a recipe for the children to follow. It reinforces their previous learning that a recipe tells the reader how to make something and helps them to appreciate the use of diagrams in making instructions clear. Remind them how this is different from a story, in which the sentences say what happened. Also discuss how the sentences are different from captions. Link this with work in design and technology on healthy eating. The children could add explanations to the instructions: for example, why the top colour is poured into the yogurt pot first and is at the bottom of the pot (the diagram helps). They could add 'so that' or 'because' clauses to the instruction sentences.	115
Do as I say Make this	**9. Creating and shaping texts** Maintain consistency in non-narrative, including purpose and tense	**All Writing AFs, especially:** **Writing AF1** Write imaginative, interesting and thoughtful texts **Writing AF2** Produce texts which are appropriate to task, reader and purpose **Writing AF7** Select appropriate and effective vocabulary	**Do as I say** develops skills in maintaining consistency in non-narrative, including purpose and tense. It provides pictures of actions and requires the children to give an instruction for someone to perform the actions. Remind them of the difference between a sentence that says what happened: for example, *I hopped on one leg*, and an instruction: for example, *Hop on one leg*. They can evaluate their instructions by comparing the action in the picture with what their friend does. If these do not match they could consider how to improve the instruction. They might need help with the vocabulary involved: for example, *raise, lift, cross-legged, cross your legs, hips, flat, stretch, straight, wink, blink, open, close*. **Make this** develops skills in maintaining consistency in non-narrative, including purpose and tense. It consolidates the children's understanding of how instructions for making things should be set out: beginning with a list of materials or equipment and then saying, step by step, what to do. To evaluate their instructions they can compare their friend's picture with the one on the card and, if appropriate, find ways of improving the instructions: for example, did they give the right name for the shape, did they say which way up it should go, did they say what size it should be, did they say whether it should go beside, below or above another shape? It may be useful to revise positional language. For added interest the children could first colour the shapes. You will need to provide cut-out shapes of the correct (and some incorrect) colours.	116 117
Treasure hunt	**9. Creating and shaping texts** Select from different presentational features to suit particular writing purposes on paper and on screen	**All Writing AFs, especially:** **Writing AF1** Write imaginative, interesting and thoughtful texts **Writing AF2** Produce texts which are appropriate to task, reader and purpose **Writing AF7** Select appropriate and effective vocabulary	**Treasure hunt** develops skills in writing for different contexts and purposes: here they decide where the treasure is to be hidden and then give step-by-step directions for finding it, using imperative verbs (this term is unlikely to be introduced except for exceptionally high-achieving children). This could be linked with work in geography on the local environment. You could take the children for a walk and, as you go, encourage them to talk about the route, and then, back in class, to convert this into directions: for example, *We turned left out of the gate and went along Sea Street/Turn left out of the gate and go along Sea Street*. This could be supported by making a map of the route, on which the children can write directions. The map could be drawn on a large sheet of paper or on screen, using whiteboard tools. The children could use glue or, on screen, drag and drop photographs into the appropriate places on the map and then write captions for them as well as writing the directions for the route.	118
Sand pie How to light a bulb	**10. Text structure and organisation** Use appropriate language to make sections hang together	**Writing AF3** Organise and present whole texts effectively, sequencing and structuring information, ideas and events **Writing AF4** Construct paragraphs and use cohesion within and between paragraphs	**Sand pie** and **How to light a light bulb** encourage the children to use planning to establish clear sections for writing and help them to use language to make sections hang together. It helps them to write instructions with care in the correct sequence. To help them to focus on the writing on p119, [on p120, they should use the diagrams to help them compose their instructions], a very simple activity has been chosen – one they will all know how to do. The questions help them to include all the relevant information.	119 120
Question mark Question queen Email check	**11. Sentence structure and punctuation** Use question marks and use commas to separate items in a list	**Writing AF5** Vary sentences for clarity, purpose and effect **Writing AF6** Write with technical accuracy of syntax and punctuation in phrases, clauses and sentences	**Question mark** and **Question queen** are about sentences which are questions. The children learn how to form a question mark and how to position it on a line of writing. It is useful to ask the children some questions and for them to answer them and then let the children ask some questions for others to answer. Draw out which sentences need full stops and which need question marks. You could point out that part of a question mark is the same as a full stop. The children could take turns to make up their own 'I want…' sentences in which they describe the items they list. **Email check** is about distinguishing between questions and other sentences. It is useful to ask the children draw out which sentences need full stops and which need question marks. You could point out that part of a question mark is the same as a full stop because it belongs at the end of a sentence. The part above the full stop shows that the sentence is a question. The children could take turns to make up their own 'I want…' sentences in which they describe the items they list. You could also provide opportunities for them to identify the appropriate punctuation keys on a keyboard.	121–122 123

Year 2 Non-Fiction unit 2 Explanations

Activity name	Strand and learning objectives	Notes on the activities	Assessment Focus	Page number
Hat test Rain hat test talk	**1. Speaking** Explain ideas and processes using imaginative and adventurous vocabulary and non-verbal gestures to support communication	**Hat test** and **Rain hat test talk** provide a context for explaining ideas. They could be used in connection with work in science – planning a fair test to find the most waterproof material and to draw attention to how results can be presented to an audience. This sheet could be adapted for an alternative, similar investigation. Encourage the children to use such a sheet to guide them in a presentation rather than using it as a script. **Vocabulary:** *cotton, fair, fleece, listen, material, polythene, pour, speak, take turns, test.*	**Speaking and listening AF1** Talk in purposeful and imaginative ways to explore ideas and feelings, adapting and varying structure and vocabulary according to purpose, listeners, and content	124–125
Make and write At home in the past On the road	**2. Listening and responding** Listen to talk by an adult, remember some specific points and identify what they have learned	**Make and write** involves listening to a presentation by an adult, remembering some specific points and identifying what has been learned. There is also an opportunity to respond to the presentation and evaluate it in terms of how easy it was to follow. The children could plan their own presentations about something they have made. You could record these using a video camera for other groups or classes to watch later. **Vocabulary:** *explain, instructions, make, materials, presentation, watch.* **At home in the past** involves listening to a talk given by an adult, remembering some specific points and identifying what has been learned. The 'house' format helps the children to record what they remember in note form so that they can refer to their notes when talking about what they learned. The activity has a natural link with work in history on homes in the past. **Vocabulary:** *a long time ago, bathroom, bedroom, cleaning, heating, kitchen, living room, past.* **On the road** provides a series of questions to focus the children's attention on specific points in a talk given by an adult, helping them to identify what they learned. It also encourages them to listen to the questions asked by others, and the answers given. Using the CD-ROM and interactive whiteboard you could let the children adapt the page, changing the questions to reflect their own queries. **Vocabulary:** *cross, crossing, pelican crossing, road safety, traffic, zebra crossing.*	**Speaking and listening AF2** Listen and respond to others, including in pairs and groups, shaping meanings through suggestions, comments, and question	126 127 128
Welcome	**3. Group discussion and interaction** Ensure everyone contributes, allocate tasks, and consider alternatives and reach agreement	**Welcome** is about taking turns to speak, listening to one another's views and preferences as the children consider the best ways of welcoming a new member of their class. This could be presented as a group activity led by an adult, with the page displayed on the interactive whiteboard and the children keying in the ideas they discuss. **Vocabulary:** *consideration, listen, preferences, views, welcome.*	**Speaking and listening AF2** Listen and respond to others, including in pairs and groups, shaping meanings through suggestions, comments, and question	129
Remember, remember	**5. Word recognition: decoding (reading) and encoding (spelling)** Read and spell less common alternative graphemes including trigraphs	**Remember, remember** helps the children to read and spell words containing less common alternative graphemes through introducing strategies to help: the use of mnemonics (both visual and verbal). Other words for which mnemonics might be useful include *build, buy, cupboard.* The children could suggest their own sentences or pictures to help them to remember the 'tricky bits' of the words. They should discuss other words they find difficult and work together on memory aids for them. Mnemonics are personal, as everyone remembers things in different ways according to their own learning style: visual, verbal and so on.	**Reading AF1** Use a range of strategies including accurate decoding of text, to read for meaning **Writing AF8** Use correct spelling	130
Plurals wordsearch Match and sort: plurals My favourite things	**6. Word structure and spelling** Spell with increasing accuracy and confidence, drawing on word recognition and knowledge of word structure, and spelling patterns including common inflections and use of double letters	**Plurals wordsearch** and **Match and sort: plurals** focus on spelling with increasing accuracy and confidence, drawing on word recognition and knowledge of word structure and spelling patterns, including common inflections. They introduce plurals; this will help the children to appreciate that many base words are changed when they mean more than one. You could introduce the term plural if appropriate. During the plenary session, invite feedback about how the words changed to mean more than one and ask the children what else we do to make a plural (add **-es**) and how we know when to do this (when a word ends in **s, x, ch** or **sh**). Point out other plural forms: for example, where the word is unchanged (*deer, fish, sheep*) or an unusual form is used (*children, men, mice, oxen, women*). **My favourite things** is about spelling with increasing accuracy and confidence, drawing on word recognition and knowledge of word structure and spelling patterns, including common inflections, and reading and spelling common alternative graphemes. The children use what they have learned from previous activities to help them to form plurals, including those where **-es** is added. It is useful to make the rules for forming plurals explicit: for example, **To make a plural we usually add s**, then ask the children what else we do to make a plural (add **-es**) *fairy/fairies, berry/berries, story/ stories;* (add **-es**) *boss/bosses, fox/foxes, witch/witches, match/matches.* Ask them to try just adding **-s** and discuss the difficulty in pronouncing the words.	**Writing AF8** Use correct spelling	131–132 133
Sail away	**6. Word structure and spelling** Read and spell less common alternative graphemes including trigraphs	**Sail away** is about spelling alternative graphemes, focussing on the **ai** phoneme. It provides an opportunity to discuss spelling rules: **ai** is rarely seen at the ends of words, where **ay** is more common; **ay** rarely occurs in the middle of words unless they are at the end of the first element of a compound word or of a word with a suffix: *daylight, haystack, payment, boyish, toybox, toytown.* Encourage the children to choose letters even if they are not sure what the words are, but discuss the correct use of graphemes and use of rules as the first approach to writing unfamiliar words.	**Writing AF8** Use correct spelling	134

Titles	Objectives	Teaching notes	Assessment focuses	Page
Dragon life cycle Fairyland Buildings glossary: 1 and 2	**7. Understanding and interpreting texts** Explain organisational features of texts, including alphabetical order, layout, diagrams, captions, hyperlinks and bullet points	**Dragon life cycle** develops the children's skills in using diagrams in explanations. Ask them to think about why the life cycle of an animal or plant is called a 'life cycle'. You could ask them where they have heard the word cycle used. Ask them what came first – the dragon or the egg. If they say 'the egg', ask where it came from and draw out that the dragon that laid it came from an egg. A group of six children could each hold an enlarged copy of a stage of the dragon's life cycle and arrange themselves in the correct order. If they arrange themselves in a straight line, help them to make links between the two ends of the line so that they form a circle. You could draw a life cycle diagram (copy and enlarge the one at the top of the page) onto which the children can glue the pictures. Before the children cut out the pictures on the sheet, discuss the instructions for the activity. Why do they think that bullet points have been used? How do they help to make the instructions easier to follow? Why aren't the captions on the cards whole sentences? In the plenary session, ask the children how the diagram makes it easier to understand what happens in a dragon's life. **Fairyland** is about the features of information texts. The children use notes presented in a fact-file to help them to complete a cloze passage about fairies. Draw out how this is different from a fairytale, which is a story about what happened. The fact-file can help to answer the question at the top of the page: information texts help us to find things out. **Buildings glossary: 1 and 2** helps the children to understand the structure of a glossary and how to use it. Introduce or revise the term *definition* and ask the children to cut out the definitions and the pictures with their captions. The cards can be used in various ways: for example, give each child a picture with a caption and then read definitions at random. The child with the picture and caption that match the definition puts up a hand to claim it. Ask each group to put their definitions in alphabetical order. If appropriate, you could then give the entire set to a group to put in alphabetical order. Discuss why a glossary is arranged in alphabetical order and how this helps. Demonstrate this by asking different groups to locate a definition in an alphabetically ordered glossary and a randomly organised glossary.	**Reading AF2** Understand, describe, select or retrieve information, events or ideas from texts and use quotation and reference to text **Reading AF3** Deduce, infer or interpret information, events or ideas from texts **Reading AF1** Use a range of strategies including accurate decoding of text, to read for meaning **Reading AF4** Identify and comment on the structure and organisation of texts, including grammatical and presentational features at text level **Reading AF5** Explain and comment on writers' uses of language, including grammatical and literary features at word and sentence level	135 136 137–138
What makes them go? Garden animals glossary	**9. Creating and shaping texts** Select from different presentational features to suit particular writing purposes on paper and on screen	**What makes them go?** develops skills in using presentational features to suit particular writing purposes on paper. It develops skills in using a chart. It should be linked with their work on pushes and pulls in science. After they have completed the chart they could use it for reference as they explain how the toys move. **Garden animals glossary** develops skills in maintaining consistency in non-narrative and in using presentational features to suit particular writing purposes on paper. It helps the children to organise a glossary in alphabetical order and to write the relevant information for each entry. They should first read some glossaries and notice their important features: alphabetical order, present tense verbs (although this term will probably not be introduced), brief and giving important facts. They could cut out the pictures and glue them onto the glossary, leaving space to write the words. They could also contribute to a larger glossary of small garden animals as they learn about them in science lessons – what makes them similar to, and different from, other animals and why they are often found in gardens. This could be created in a table using two columns and arranging the words in alphabetical order using the 'sort' facility. This is useful for adding items to a glossary, since new rows can be added either at the end or in their correct alphabetical place.	**All Writing AFs, especially:** **Writing AF1** Write imaginative, interesting and thoughtful texts **Writing AF2** Produce texts which are appropriate to task, reader and purpose **Writing AF7** Select appropriate and effective vocabulary	139 140
Making music What sank the boat?	**10. Text structure and organisation** Use planning to establish clear sections for writing	**Making music** encourages the children to use planning to establish clear sections for writing and helps them to use language to make sections hang together. It develops skills in using charts. This time they are provided with a blank chart and asked to supply their own heading (for a less challenging activity, insert the headings *shake, tap, scrape* and *blow*. Link this with work in music and science (light and sound). You could also create a chart on a computer and display it on an interactive whiteboard (or on paper or a display board). Provide photographs taken using a digital camera or scanned from brochures and ask the children to label them and drag them into the appropriate columns and, if necessary, add columns: for example, *pluck*. **What sank the boat?** encourages the children to use planning to establish clear sections for writing. It helps them to structure an explanation using logical connectives. It is useful to link this with their investigations – in science lessons. To help them to organise the explanation, they are asked to write a sentence about each picture – in the order in which the pictures are presented. You could display the pictures on an electronic whiteboard. To introduce the activity, the story *Who Sank the Boat?* by Pamela Allen (Puffin) provides some useful discussion points. You could model how to complete the first two sentences and point out how they are different from a recount (a recount would say what happened but not what made it happen). *Explanation:* The boat hit a rock. This made a hole in the boat. So water got into the boat. This made the boat sink. The dog jumped into the boat. This made the boat go down at one end. So water filled the boat. This made the boat fill with water and sink.	**Writing AF3** Organise and present whole texts effectively, sequencing and structuring information, ideas and events **Writing AF4** Construct paragraphs and use cohesion within and between paragraphs	141 142
What for? Tell me why Sentence robots	**11. Sentence structure and punctuation** Write simple and compound sentences and begin to use subordination in relation to time and reason	**What for?** and **Tell me why** requires the children to consider how to extend simple sentences to form complex sentences involving subordination by using the connectives *so* and *because* to indicate purpose. You could also read out simple sentences beginning with an action which can be followed by a purpose and invite volunteers to add to them using *to* or *because*, followed by an ending which says what the character did the action for. Write up the sentences for the children to reread later. It is useful to remind them that each sentence begins with a capital letter and ends with a full stop. Also remind them that a sentence can go past the end of a line. **Sentence robots** provides practice in writing simple sentences. You could add an extra challenge by timing this activity. Set an appropriate time target for the children (this could be varied within the class for children working at different levels). Some children could be asked to say what questions the sentence answer (*Who or what did it?, What did they do?* and *Where?*).	**Writing AF5** Vary sentences for clarity, purpose and effect **Writing AF6** Write with technical accuracy of syntax and punctuation in phrases, clauses and sentences	143–144 145

Year 2 Non-Fiction unit 3 Information texts

Activity name	Strand and learning objectives	Notes on the activities	Assessment Focus	Page number
That's the way to make it: 1 and 2 / What am I doing? / Wordless	**1. Speaking** Explain ideas and processes using imaginative and adventurous vocabulary and non-verbal gestures to support communication	**That's the way to make it: 1 and 2** encourage the children to talk about processes. They also support work on writing and following instructions. While making the peanut butter (or other spread) roll they might discover useful tips to pass on to the audience, such as how much spread to use or how to stop it squeezing out of the sides of the roll. While making the orange jelly, the children might find a way to use the flesh as well as the juice of the orange, how to scrape it out and what to do if there is not enough juice to top up the liquid needed for the jelly. Different groups could prepare different foods and present the instructions as if they are TV chefs. They could even make video recordings of themselves as 'TV chefs' with one introducing the programme and the others taking turns to explain parts of the process, including any tips they want to add. **Vocabulary:** *explain, instructions, listen, make, pour, recipe, roll, spread, tell, watch.* **What am I doing?** and **Wordless** support the use of non-verbal gestures in communication. The children mime an activity for their group or the class to identify. No speaking is allowed: they are required to communicate entirely through actions. You could 'think aloud' about the actions to do: for example, *I'm going to mime reading a book, so first I'll get my glasses out of their case and put them on, then I'll look at some books on a shelf and choose one. I'll look at the front and back cover and open the book; then I'll sit down and read it.* Also model how to exaggerate these actions and 'act' them. **Vocabulary:** *act, actions, exaggerate, mime.*	**Speaking and listening AF1** Talk in purposeful and imaginative ways to explore ideas and feelings, adapting and varying structure and vocabulary according to purpose, listeners, and content	146–147 / 148–149
Mary Seacole / Holiday talk	**2. Listening and responding** Listen to talk by an adult, remember some specific points and identify what they have learned	**Mary Seacole** involves listening to a talk and remembering specific points. An adult could read the following text to the children and allow some time for them to ask questions: Mary Seacole was born in Jamaica about 200 years ago. Her mother was a doctress – a woman who cared for sick or injured people. Mary used to help her mother and learned a lot from her. When she grew up she wanted to be a nurse. She had heard about the famous nurse Florence Nightingale and wanted to do the same kind of work. She sailed to England to see if she could join Florence Nightingale's nurses and go to the war in the Crimea – a place close to the Black Sea. The officials in London told her that they did not need any more nurses. Mary was very disappointed. She was sure that the army would be glad of another nurse to look after the wounded soldiers. She had read in the newspapers about the poor food and the cold, uncomfortable camps the soldiers lived in. She made up her mind to pay her own fare to sail to the Crimea and help. She went by steamship – a long slow journey – with stores of food, equipment to set up a kitchen and many useful things to sell. When Mary got to the Crimea she built a big hut. This was to be her shop and café. Travellers and the soldiers who could afford it used to eat there. Whenever there was a battle Mary would walk to the battlefield with her stove and kettle to make tea for the soldiers. She also carried her first aid kit so that she could treat their wounds. Mary's hut became known as 'Mother Seacole's Hut'. The soldiers called her 'Mother Seacole' because she looked after them like a mother. Before long Mary built a bigger place, which she named 'The British Hotel'. Army officers and their wives went to stay there and it became known for its good food. Mary still went to the battlefields to care for the wounded soldiers. Once she had to fling herself onto the ground face down to stay safe from bullets. After the war was over Mary sailed to England. She had no money left. The soldiers wanted to do something to thank Mary for her care so they held a big festival in London to raise money for her. **Vocabulary:** *army, Black Sea, Crimea, equipment, Jamaica, journey, medicine, nurse, soldiers, steamship, war, wounds.* **Holiday talk** supports the children in remembering some specific points when listening to a talk given by an adult and helps them to identify what they have learned. This could be linked with work in geography (Where in the world is Barnaby Bear?). It also supports work on Responding to texts (making brief notes that can be read later). **Vocabulary:** *fact, important, holiday, journey, listen, notes.*	**Speaking and listening AF2** Listen and respond to others, including in pairs and groups, shaping meanings through suggestions, comments, and question	150 / 151
That's good / That's bad	**3. Group discussion and interaction** Listen to each others views and preferences, agree the next steps to take and identify contributions by each group member	**That's good** and **That's bad** focus on listening to one another's views and preferences and ensuring that everyone contributes to a discussion. This could be presented as a group activity led by an adult, with the page displayed on the interactive whiteboard and the children keying in the ideas they discuss; or give the children time to reflect individually on what is meant by good or bad, ask them to make a note of their ideas and then talk to one another about these. Completing the page as a group requires them to reach agreement. **Vocabulary:** *consideration, listen, preferences, right, views, wrong.*	**Speaking and listening AF2** Listen and respond to others, including in pairs and groups, shaping meanings through suggestions, comments, and question	152–153
The chest	**4. Drama** Adopt appropriate roles in small or large groups and consider alternative courses of action	**The chest.** Ask the children to imagine they are opening the chest. What do they see, hear and smell? Can they communicate this to an audience through speaking to one another, rather than telling a story as narrators? **Vocabulary:** *act, audience, imagine, role.*	**Speaking and listening AF3** Create and sustain different roles and scenarios, adapting techniques to explore texts, ideas, and issues	154
Word partners	**5. Word recognition: decoding (reading) and encoding (spelling)** Read and spell less common alternative graphemes including trigraphs	**Word partners** develops skills to aid independent reading and spelling with increased accuracy, drawing on word recognition and word structure. It introduces compound words (this term need not be introduced). The children should be able to use phonics to read the individual words from which compound words can be made. Suggest that the children shade each card set in a different colour before cutting them out to avoid confusing the two sets. The cut-out cards can be used in different ways.	**Reading AF1** Use a range of strategies including accurate decoding of text, to read for meaning **Writing AF8** Use correct spelling	155

Resource	Objective	Teaching notes	Assessment Focus	Page
Oil the toy	**6. Word structure and spelling** Read and spell less common alternative graphemes including trigraphs	**Oil the toy** is about spelling alternative graphemes, focussing on **/oi/** phonemes. It provides an opportunity to discuss spelling rules: **/oi/** is rarely seen at the ends of words, where **oy** is more common; **oy** rarely occurs in the middle of words unless it is at the end of the first element of a compound word or a word with a suffix: *boyish, toybox, toytown*. Encourage the children to choose letters even if they are not sure what the words are, but discuss the correct use of graphemes and use of rules as the first approach to writing unfamiliar words.	**Writing AF8** Use correct spelling	156
Miss Muffet's friends	**7. Understanding and interpreting texts** Explain organisational features of texts, including alphabetical order, layout, diagrams, captions, hyperlinks and bullet points	**Miss Muffet's friends** helps the children to understand the structure of an alphabetically ordered text and how to use it. Explain that names are usually listed by family name rather than personal name. Some children might need to use an alphabet strip and to match the names to the letters. They could also make their own address books and enter the names and addresses of their friends. Link this with work on capital letters and with work in geography on streets, towns, countries and different kinds of maps.	**Reading AF2** Understand, describe, select or retrieve information, events or ideas from texts and use quotation and reference to text **Reading AF3** Deduce, infer or interpret information, events or ideas from texts **Reading AF1** Use a range of strategies including accurate decoding of text, to read for meaning **Reading AF4** Identify and comment on the structure and organisation of texts, including grammatical and presentational features at text level **Reading AF5** Explain and comment on writers' uses of language, including grammatical and literary features at word and sentence level	157
Fairytale facts		**Fairytale facts** helps the children to use an alphabetically ordered text to find information. Some of them could also enter the names of their class (or a section of the class on a table in Word) and use the 'Sort' command in the menu to put them in order. Ask them how it sorted those beginning with the same letter. You could also provide a random list of words and an alphabetically ordered list and let the children investigate which is the easier to use. They could write their full names on slips of paper and arrange them in alphabetical order of personal name and then family name.		158
Homes in the past web page Toys in the past web links Seaside web links	**9. Creating and shaping texts** Select from different presentational features to suit particular writing purposes on paper and on screen	**Homes in the past web page**, **Toys in the past web links** and **Seaside web links** provide opportunities for the children to select from presentational features to suit particular writing purposes on paper and on screen. They encourage them to draw on knowledge and experience of information texts to help them to write their own. It links with work in ICT and history as it helps them to plan hyperlinks to add to an information text about homes in the past, toys in the past or the seaside in the past. The children should use information books to find the information they need, write simple notes and then build them into sentences for the links. If possible and with appropriate adult help, children could see their material linked in a set of web links (perhaps on the school website).	**All Writing AFs, especially:** **Writing AF1** Write imaginative, interesting and thoughtful texts **Writing AF2** Produce texts which are appropriate to task, reader and purpose **Writing AF7** Select appropriate and effective vocabulary	159–161
Fruit: 1, 2 and 3	**10. Text structure and organisation** Use planning to establish clear sections for writing	**Fruit: 1**, **Fruit: 2** and **Fruit: 3** encourage the children to use planning to establish clear sections for writing and help them to maintain consistency in non-narrative, developing skills in organising information about a subject in a way that groups it according to similarities. Here they group a collection of fruits according to the type of plant they come from. This encourages them to use information texts to find out what they need to know and to write simple notes (for example, key words and phrases and page/web references) to use in their own writing. There is an obvious link with work in science on variation. First give pairs of children a copy of **Fruit: 1** (page 162) and ask them to cut out and sort the fruits into sets that have similarities. Let them choose how to do this and then invite feedback. They are likely to use observable characteristics such as shape or characteristics they know about if they are familiar with the fruits. Then help them to use the Internet, CDs and information books (and some examples of the fruits themselves) to find the information they need to complete the chart on **Fruit: 2** (page 163). Different groups could find out about different fruits. **Fruit: 3** (page 164) helps them to plan a shared information book that includes all the fruits. Encourage the groups to share its findings with the others so that each group can complete its own contents page to help them to organise the book, which could later be completed as a collaborative activity with different children writing about different fruits, or compiling an information book or e-book about fruit.	**Writing AF3** Organise and present whole texts effectively, sequencing and structuring information, ideas and events **Writing AF4** Construct paragraphs and use cohesion within and between paragraphs	162–164
But	**11. Sentence structure and punctuation** Write simple and compound sentences and begin to use subordination in relation to time and reason	**But** introduces the connective word *but*. The children learn to link two simple sentences with *but* to form a compound sentence. You could also read out simple sentences and invite volunteers to add to them using *but*. Write up the sentences for the children to reread later.	**Writing AF5** Vary sentences for clarity, purpose and effect **Writing AF6** Write with technical accuracy of syntax and punctuation in phrases, clauses and sentences	165
Then		**Then** introduces the connective word *then*. The children learn to link two simple sentences with *then* to form a compound sentence. It is useful to point out that the name of the person doing the action is not usually repeated; for example, *She ate a cake and (she) drank some tea, We saw a flash of light and (we) heard a loud bang.* You could also read out simple sentences and invite volunteers to add to them using *then*. Write up the sentences for the children to reread later.		166
Tell me when		**Tell me when** is about words indicating time. Remind the children of the questions they have been asked when building sentences in their previous work: *Who (or what) did the action? What did they do?, Where?, When? and Why?* You could also show the children the class timetable and help them to compose sentences about when specific activities are carried out.		167
Question time	**11. Sentence structure and punctuation** Use question marks and use commas to separate items in a list	**Question time** focuses on changing a sentence into a question. In addition to exchanging the full stop for a question mark, the children learn how to alter the order of the words to make a sentence into a question.	**Writing AF5** Vary sentences for clarity, purpose and effect **Writing AF6** Write with technical accuracy of syntax and punctuation in phrases, clauses and sentences	168
The comma		**The comma** shows the children how to form a list without a comma. You could demonstrate how it is used by reading a list without a comma and encourage them to follow the text with a finger and pause at each comma as you pause slightly during the reading.		169

Year 2 Non-Fiction unit 4 Non-chronological reports

Activity name	Strand and learning objectives	Notes on the activities	Assessment Focus	Page number
Play the game Play the game questions A new game	**1. Speaking** Explain ideas and processes using imaginative and adventurous vocabulary and non-verbal gestures to support communication	**Play the game. Play the game questions** and **A new game** develop skills in speaking to a small group to explain a process using non-verbal gestures to support verbal communication. The game can be introduced by inviting the children to talk about other 'circle' games they play: for example, 'The Farmer's in his Den'. Ask them how the players are chosen for a turn at the main activity of the game (such as stepping into the centre of the circle, running or skipping or passing a ball or other object), how their turn ends and the next player's turn begins and how the game ends. When they answer, encourage them to speak to the group rather than just to the teacher and to look them. They could check their own understanding of the game by answering the questions on page 171. These questions could also be answered by the children they told how to play. Draw out the main features of the game: a player skips or runs round the others, who form a circle; he or she carries an object and drops it behind one of the others, who chases him or her and, if successful, is the next one to skip round the circle. The words for the rhyme *Lucy Locket* are given on page 178. **Vocabulary:** *choose, circle, drop, sing, start, stop.*	**Speaking and listening AF1** Talk in purposeful and imaginative ways to explore ideas and feelings, adapting and varying structure and vocabulary according to purpose, listeners, and content	170-172
In the groove	**5. Word recognition:** decoding (reading) and encoding (spelling) Read high and medium frequency words independently and automatically	**In the groove** helps the children to spell high frequency and topic words by developing their ability to identify potentially difficult elements in words. The focus here is on words ending with the phoneme /**v**/, which is almost always spelled **ve**. Very few words end with **v**. The cards can also be used for 'Matching pairs' or 'Find your partner'.	**Reading AF1** Use a range of strategies including accurate decoding of text, to read for meaning **Writing AF8** Use correct spelling	173
Worker words	**6. Word structure and spelling** Spell with increasing accuracy and confidence, drawing on word recognition and knowledge of word structure, and spelling patterns including common inflections and use of double letters	**Base words with -ful** is about spelling with increasing accuracy and confidence, drawing on word recognition and knowledge of word structure and spelling patterns, including common inflections. Note that few base words change when **-ful** is added: most of those that change end in **ll** or **y**: for example, *skill/skilful, duty/dutiful, fancy/fanciful, bounty/bountiful* and *beauty/beautiful.*	**Writing AF8** Use correct spelling	174
Island reports Island fact-file Note it	**7. Understanding and interpreting texts** Explain organisational features of texts, including alphabetical order, layout, diagrams, captions, hyperlinks and bullet points	**Island reports** is about using different types of information text to find out about an island. It focuses on literacy skills in the context of geography (An island home). Choose an island to investigate: for example, Coll (see below) and collect a leaflet or travel brochure, a book and details of a website. Show the children the three texts and ask them how they are similar. Ask them what is different about them: for example, the amount of text and pictures, how to find pages, the number of pages, how they are set out: where the headings, pictures, diagrams and captions are arranged. Show them how to locate the contents/menu of each text (if it has one) and ask them what they think they will find in the text: for example, photographs of the island, sound recordings, videos, panoramic views, interactive quizzes. During the plenary session, ask the children which text they enjoyed using the most and what they liked about it and which was the most useful, and why. This activity could be linked with reading the Katie Morag stories by Mairi Hedderwick (Random House), set on the imaginary island of Struay (based on the author's home on the island of Coll in the Hebrides). Useful websites you could use are: http://www.isle-of-man.com/, http://www.iwight.com/, http://www.lindisfarne.org.uk/ and http://www.visitanglesey.com/. **Island fact-file** develops from the activity on page 183. Having discovered what a website contains, the children use it to find specific information. Model how to scan the menu or site map and 'think aloud' about the headings and pictures and whether they will provide information about the landscape, coast and buildings: for example, 'This button says Shoreline. That means coast, so it will tell me about the seashores around the island. It might even show pictures of them.' The children could use books or brochures to find the same information and say which they found the easiest, and why. **Note it** develops skills in making and reading notes. The chart provides a model for note-making. It could be adapted for recording other investigations in science. The emphasis here is on interpreting a chart in order to find information to answer questions. Point out the key and, if necessary, explain it. As an extension activity the children could write another question for a friend to answer using the chart. You could write questions for the children to answer using notes they have made on a chart about another investigation.	**Reading AF2** Understand, describe, select or retrieve information, events or ideas from texts and use quotation and reference to text **Reading AF3** Deduce, infer or interpret information, events or ideas from texts **Reading AF1** Use a range of strategies including accurate decoding of text, to read for meaning **Reading AF4** Identify and comment on the structure and organisation of texts, including grammatical and presentational features at text level **Reading AF5** Explain and comment on writers' uses of language, including grammatical and literary features at word and sentence level	175 176 177
Double page plan Dinosaur report	**9. Creating and shaping texts** Select from different presentational features to suit particular writing purposes on paper and on screen	**Double page plan** encourages the children to use planning to establish clear sections for writing and to select from presentational features to suit particular writing purposes. It develops their awareness of the way in which information in a non-chronological report is presented on the page: headings, sub-headings, illustrations, captions and the main body of the text. They could use this plan for a paper-based or ICT-based non-chronological report on any subject. **Dinosaur report** helps the children to draw on knowledge and experience of non-chronological reports in planning and to select from presentational features to suit the purpose. It develops their awareness of the way in which information in a non-chronological report is sequenced: an introduction followed by information grouped according to sense or meaning. Here the dinosaurs can be grouped according to diet. Ask children to decide what the title of each chapter should be.	**All Writing AFs, especially:** **Writing AF1** Write imaginative, interesting and thoughtful texts **Writing AF2** Produce texts which are appropriate to task, reader and purpose **Writing AF7** Select appropriate and effective vocabulary	178 179

Activity name	Strand and learning objectives	Notes on the activities	Assessment Focus	Page number
Habitats plan Two habitats Paragraphs	**10. Text structure and organisation** Use planning to establish clear sections for writing	**Habitats plan** encourages the children to use planning to establish clear sections for writing. It provides a mind-map format to help them to bring to mind what they already know about habitats in the school grounds and to organise this in a way that will help them to plan a non-chronological report about these habitats. They could use the main words in the ovals as sub-headings and link them to plants and animals they know can be found there. Children could add their own bubbles if they can think of more habitats than there are printed bubbles. **Two habitats** helps the children to use planning to establish clear sections for writing. The children first need to have read some non-chronological reports and should know what is meant by a paragraph. They organise the notes they make about two habitats in the school grounds (or other local area) and to write a paragraph on a theme within this topic. The organisation of their notes will help them to structure a nonchronological report about habitats. Different groups could focus on different habitats identified during their work on Habitats plan (page 180). **Paragraphs** develops skills in using planning to establish clear sections for writing. It is about organising ideas into general themes, key details and information. Some children might need help in separating the text into paragraphs: if so, ask them to make a paragraph for the introduction and a separate paragraph for each different type of fairy.	**Writing AF3** Organise and present whole texts effectively, sequencing and structuring information, ideas and events **Writing AF4** Construct paragraphs and use cohesion within and between paragraphs	180 181 182

Year 2 Poetry unit 1 Patterns on the page

Activity name	Strand and learning objectives	Notes on the activities	Assessment Focus	Page number
A poem to read aloud: 1 and 2	**1. Speaking** Speak with clarity and use appropriate intonation when reading and reciting texts	**A poem to read aloud: 1** and **2** focus on speaking clearly and using intonation when reading. Model how to read the fast parts of 'A Lazy Thought' in a rushed way and to contrast the slow part, using the sounds of the words to create these effects. The children could make lists of 'fast' and 'slow' words: for example, (fast) *darting, dashing, racing, running, rushing, scurrying*; (slow) *amble, glide, slide, stretch, stroll*. This could also be used to support drama: the children could enact the scene after planning it, with help: rushing to get to a destination, pushing their way through crowds, being squashed into a train or bus in the rush hour and then the contrasting slow actions: stretching out, playing, chatting. They should read 'O Dandelion' so that it sounds like questions and answers. The children could make up some questions and answers for another flower: for example, a sunflower or poppy. **Vocabulary:** *crush, expression, flurry, rush, scurry, slow.*	**Speaking and listening AF1** Talk in purposeful and imaginative ways to explore ideas and feelings, adapting and varying structure and vocabulary according to purpose, listeners, and content	183–184
Laughometer	**2. Listening and responding** Respond to presentations by describing characters, repeating some highlights and commenting constructively	**Laughometer** provides an opportunity for the children to respond to presentations and to comment constructively. Invite feedback after they have each read their joke to their group and discussed which ones they found funny, and why, and recorded their results on the 'laughometer'. Did every group find the same jokes funny? Were the jokes themselves the funniest or was it the way in which they were told? Invite volunteers to tell jokes to the class. Discuss what made them laugh. The children could also collect their own jokes. Before copying the sheet, you could use the CD-ROM to substitute other jokes, etc. Link this with work on Engaging with and responding to texts (Silly stuff). **Vocabulary:** *audience, comment, joke, laugh, listen, tell, voice.*	**Speaking and listening AF2** Listen and respond to others, including in pairs and groups, shaping meanings through suggestions, comments, and question	185
Cold hands	**3. Group discussion and interaction** Work effectively in groups by ensuring that each group member takes a turn challenging, supporting and moving on	**Cold hands** develops skills in working effectively in a group by ensuring that each member takes a turn in challenging, supporting and moving on. If possible, you could provide examples of different gloves or materials to support the children. You could adapt the page using the CD-ROM to replace the fictitious teacher with one the children know and invite them to help him or her to choose some new gloves. Link this with work in science on materials. **Vocabulary:** *agreement, cotton, decide, fleece, listen, material, opinion, plan, sheepskin, test, warm, woollen.*	**Speaking and listening AF2** Listen and respond to others, including in pairs and groups, shaping meanings through suggestions, comments, and question	186
The Jolly Hunter	**3. Group discussion and interaction** Listen to each others views and preferences, agree the next steps to take and identify contributions by each group member	**The Jolly Hunter** invites the children to discuss a difficult topic in a way that ensures that all views are listened to and considered, even if children disagree strongly with one another's views. You could display the page on the interactive whiteboard and invite the children to underline the word that is used the most often (Jolly) and ask if they think it is a jolly poem, and why or why not. Groups could also talk about whether it is right or wrong to shoot animals and consider the reasons for the different views. It is important to acknowledge that all their views are valid and important even if they disagree very strongly. The activity could be linked with work in citizenship on Animals and us. **Vocabulary:** *agree, contribute, cruel, deserve, disagree, hunter, right, shoot, valid, views, wrong.*	**Speaking and listening AF2** Listen and respond to others, including in pairs and groups, shaping meanings through suggestions, comments, and question	187
On stage	**4. Drama** Consider how mood or atmosphere are created in live or recorded performance	**On stage.** This activity could be used after a school play or a visit to a theatre. Discuss how the characters interacted with one another. How did this affect the performance and the audience? **Vocabulary:** *act, audience, describe, exciting, feeling, funny, lighting, lively, music, mysterious, play, quiet, scary, scenery, setting.*	**Speaking and listening AF4** Understand the range and uses of spoken language, commenting on meaning and impact and draw on this when talking to others	188

Activity name	Strand and learning objectives	Notes on the activities	Assessment Focus	Page number
Sea song	**7. Understanding and interpreting texts** Explore how particular words are used, including words and expressions with similar meanings	**Sea song** is about rhyming patterns and repeated language. After reading the first verse and the first two lines of the second verse, the children should realise that each verse begins *Sea-shell, sea-shell*, and that this is followed by a line which is repeated (*Murmuring sand, Murmuring sand*) and that in each verse these two lines rhyme with *sand: land, hand, understand*. Read the entire poem, stopping for the children to continue where there is a gap. They could later make up their own poems based on this structure, beginning, for example, with *Seagull, seagull, Cries in the air. Cries in the air.*	**Reading AF2** Understand, describe, select or retrieve information, events or ideas from texts and use quotation and reference to text **Reading AF3** Deduce, infer or interpret information, events or ideas from texts **Reading AF1** Use a range of strategies including accurate decoding of text, to read for meaning **Reading AF4** Identify and comment on the structure and organisation of texts, including grammatical and presentational features at text level **Reading AF5** Explain and comment on writers' uses of language, including grammatical and literary features at word and sentence level	189
Shoe chant	**9. Creating and shaping texts** Make adventurous word and language choices appropriate to style and purpose of text	**Shoe chant** encourages the children to draw on their knowledge and experience of chants in deciding and planning what to write. It is about writing verses for a simple chant poem that follows a particular pattern. To help them to appreciate the rhythm of this poem, read 'Bug Chant' by Tony Mitton (*The Works*, Paul Cookson, Macmillan). The children could take turns to read their verses as part of a long chant poem.	**All Writing AFs, especially: Writing AF1** Write imaginative, interesting and thoughtful texts **Writing AF2** Produce texts which are appropriate to task, reader and purpose **Writing AF7** Select appropriate and effective vocabulary	190
Sentence link	**11. Sentence structure and punctuation** Write simple and compound sentences and begin to use subordination in relation to time and reason	**Sentence link** reinforces the children's learning about how to join simple sentences to make compound sentences and complex sentences involving subordination. They are required to choose the most appropriate connective word. The children could also collect examples of sentences containing *and, but, then, because* or *to* from their reading. **That's silly** helps the children to write humorous sentences by providing beginnings and endings they can match up. This activity encourages them to think about the way in which the sentence makes sense as they are required to think about the grammatical match of beginning to ending; for example *Two old octopuses could not be followed by and brushed.*	**Writing AF5** Vary sentences for clarity, purpose and effect **Writing AF6** Write with technical accuracy of syntax and punctuation in phrases, clauses and sentences	191
That's silly				192

Year 2 Poetry unit 2 Really looking

Activity name	Strand and learning objectives	Notes on the activities	Assessment Focus	Page number
Loud and quiet	**1. Speaking** Speak with clarity and use appropriate intonation when reading and reciting texts	**Loud and quiet** is about using intonation. It focuses on changing the volume of the voice to communicate a hush: for example, when Gregg is creeping along the passage not wanting his aunt and uncle to hear him, or a louder tone when he calls out to them from upstairs and they respond. The children could also change the speed at which they read in order to communicate suspense. **Vocabulary:** *loud, quiet, tone.*	**Speaking and listening AF1** Talk in purposeful and imaginative ways to explore ideas and feelings, adapting and varying structure and vocabulary according to purpose, listeners, and content	193
On wheels: the vehicles	**3. Group discussion and interaction** Ensure everyone contributes, allocate tasks, and consider alternatives and reach agreement	**On wheels: the vehicles** and **On wheels: the drivers** present a task that requires the children to listen to one another's views and to ensure that everyone contributes. They could begin by talking about what each driver does, what he or she will carry in the vehicle, how the driver might use it and the types of places he or she will go to. They should also discuss the characteristics of each vehicle: speed, size, seating, space for goods, terrains it is suited to and how it might cope with different weather conditions. **Vocabulary:** *driver, electrician, farmer, Formula 1, landrover, learner, listen, people carrier, racing driver, saloon, terrain, transit, motorbike, vehicle.*	**Speaking and listening AF2** Listen and respond to others, including in pairs and groups, shaping meanings through suggestions, comments, and question	194–195
On wheels: the drivers				
Setting the scene	**4. Drama** Consider how mood or atmosphere are created in live or recorded performance	**Setting the scene** focuses on how mood and atmosphere are created in a recorded performance and encourages the children to consider how they can create the effects they want. Provide a selection of music for children to classify as scary, funny, exciting or romantic (link this with work in music lessons). **Vocabulary:** *introduction, lighting, lights, music, romantic, scene, setting.*	**Speaking and listening AF4** Understand the range and uses of spoken language, commenting on meaning and impact and draw on this when talking to others	196

Activity name	Strand and learning objectives	Notes on the activities	Assessment Focus	Page number
Quiet poems: 1 and 2 Words and pictures Rough or smooth	**7. Understanding and interpreting texts** Explore how particular words are used, including words and expressions with similar meanings	**Quiet poems: 1** and **2** present two poems about lying in bed at night, listening. The first has no rhyme. It has a very slow, gentle pace; the words and their layout urge the reader to read slowly and quietly. The second poem has some rhyme but no regular rhyming pattern. The effect is to slow the reading, as for the first poem. Encourage the children to notice the sounds which occur the most often in these two poems: *s, z* and *sh* (*stars, switched, still, sleeping, except; shhhhhhhhh, eyelashes, stroking, breeze, whispers, trees*) and *l* (*listen, lie, still, sleeping, eyelashes*). **Words and pictures** encourages awareness of the pictures a poem conjures up in the mind. The focus is on how sounds can create images such as a beating drum, a fastmoving train, a tiptoeing child and whizzing and whooshing fireworks. For some children will be able to complete the extension activity independently; for others this could be a shared writing activity. You could provide a video recording of an event with noticeable sounds and rhythm: part of a football match, playtime at school, waves crashing onto a shore, a horse galloping, birds flying, bees buzzing around flowers and so on. Ask the children to suggest words to describe the pictures they see: write these in a word-bank and add some of your own. **Rough or smooth** focuses on the quality of sounds. It helps the children to appreciate how the sounds of words can create an effect. Other words to consider include: *clatter, crash, flashing, flow, glide, luminous, ragged, snag*.	**Reading AF2** Understand, describe, select or retrieve information, events or ideas from texts and use quotation and reference to text **Reading AF3** Deduce, infer or interpret information, events or ideas from texts **Reading AF1** Use a range of strategies including accurate decoding of text, to read for meaning **Reading AF4** Identify and comment on the structure and organisation of texts, including grammatical and presentational features at text level **Reading AF5** Explain and comment on writers' uses of language, including grammatical and literary features at word and sentence level	197–198 199 200
Caterpillar Cat watch Rain	**9. Creating and shaping texts** Make adventurous word and language choices appropriate to style and purpose of text	**Caterpillar** helps the children to make adventurous word choices appropriate to the style of a poem. Link this with work in science on variation. They develop their vocabulary to describe a caterpillar they have closely observed and discussed and choose the most appropriate words to describe it in order to prepare for writing a descriptive poem that captures the appearance, feel and movement of a caterpillar. Make sure children do not touch caterpillars while working on this page as some produce material that irritates the skin. **Cat watch** helps the children to make adventurous word choices appropriate to the style of a poem. They develop vocabulary to describe a cat they have closely observed and discussed and choose the most appropriate words to describe it in order to prepare for writing a descriptive poem that evokes the sleek appearance of a cat and its silent slinking movements. Children could work in pairs and compose their poems aloud. Teachers could also ask children to think about patterns and rhythms, such as placing a verb at the end of each line/phrase: for example, *low purring, slow slinking*. **Rain** helps the children to make adventurous word choices appropriate to the style of a poem. They develop vocabulary to describe a shower of rain they have closely observed and discussed as they choose the most appropriate words to describe it. This prepares them in order for writing a descriptive poem that communicates the wetness and splashing sounds of the rain.	**All Writing AFs, especially:** **Writing AF1** Write imaginative, interesting and thoughtful texts **Writing AF2** Produce texts which are appropriate to task, reader and purpose **Writing AF7** Select appropriate and effective vocabulary	201 202 203

Year 2 Poetry unit 3 Silly stuff

Activity name	Strand and learning objectives	Notes on the activities	Assessment Focus	Page number
Sounds right	**1. Speaking** Speak with clarity and use appropriate intonation when reading and reciting texts	**Sounds right** is about speaking clearly and using intonation when reading. Invite volunteers to demonstrate how they would say the words. Draw attention to the different tones of voice of the characters in the pictures. You could also scan pictures of people speaking from newspapers or magazines and display them on the interactive whiteboard. Ask the children if they can tell from the person's expression, gestures and actions what kind of thing he or she might be saying: for example, giving an order or command, asking a question, accusing. Also ask what feelings the person is showing and how they can tell. **Vocabulary:** *asking, complaining, enticing, gesture, sound, telling off, sternly, tone of voice*.	**Speaking and listening AF1** Talk in purposeful and imaginative ways to explore ideas and feelings, adapting and varying structure and vocabulary according to purpose, listeners, and content	204
Fixing the wheels on	**3. Group discussion and interaction** Ensure everyone contributes, allocate tasks, and consider alternatives and reach agreement	**Fixing the wheels on** focuses on working effectively as a group. The children should listen to one another's ideas, ensuring that all have a chance to speak and are listened to equally. You could also model how to encourage others to join in in a discussion by asking them a question that does not require yes or no as an answer. Also model how to ensure that no one dominates the discussion by summing up what they have said and inviting someone who has not yet contributed to speak: for example, *So, Ben, you think the car needs wheels. What do you think about the axles? Where do the axles go? How are the axles fixed on? What about you, Callum?* **Vocabulary:** *axle, card, chassis, dowel, materials, sellotape, straws, string, triangle, turn, wheel.*	**Speaking and listening AF2** Listen and respond to others, including in pairs and groups, shaping meanings through suggestions, comments, and question	205
All in all Word addition	**6. Word structure and spelling** Spell with increasing accuracy and confidence, drawing on word recognition and knowledge of word structure, and spelling patterns including common inflections and use of double letters	**All in all** focuses on spelling with increasing accuracy and confidence, drawing on word recognition and knowledge of word structure and spelling patterns. It concentrates on using the prefix **al-** with the meaning all, fully or completely. The children will have come across the **al** grapheme for the /**or**/ phoneme during their earlier work on Phase Five of Letters and Sounds. **Word addition** develops skills to aid independent reading and spelling with increased accuracy, drawing on word recognition and word structure and less common alternative graphemes, including trigraphs. It builds on the previous activity, which introduced compound words. Other useful compound words include: *anteater, bookcase, classroom, eyebrow, eyelid, footstep, frogspawn, grapefruit, greenhouse, handwriting, handwritten, highlight, makeup, mousetrap, nutcracker, pineapple, rosebud, sandcastle, seashore, seaside, seaweed, shellfish, suntan.*	**Writing AF8** Use correct spelling	206 207

23

Wild words	**Wild words** is about describing words. As the children complete it, encourage them to read the phrases aloud, to listen to the sounds of the words and to imagine the pictures they conjure up.	**Reading AF2** Understand, describe, select or retrieve information, events or ideas from texts and use quotation and reference to text	208
A funny little man	**A funny little man** provides an opportunity to have fun with a nonsense rhyme and to enjoy its silliness. Discuss the rhyming pattern: end rhyme, then internal rhyme. The children could highlight these parts of the first verse to help them to recognise the pattern. They could make up their own verses during any spare moments. Let them explore these with a friend and recite them to the class.	**Reading AF3** Deduce, infer or interpret information, events or ideas from texts	209
Mrs Brown went up to town	**Mrs Brown went to town** presents a silly story/song. Sing it with the children and let them sing it with a friend and improvise on the verses or add their own. The only rule to follow is to keep to the rhyming pattern and the rhythm (you could show the children how to count the beats or syllables of the lines) and that the new verses have to be nonsense. They will also have to make up names for the last line.	**Reading AF1** Use a range of strategies including accurate decoding of text, to read for meaning. **Reading AF4** Identify and comment on the structure and organisation of texts, including grammatical and presentational features at text level	210
Tongue-twister match-up	**Tongue-twister match-up** develops an appreciation of alliteration. After the children have matched up the two parts of each tongue-twister, ask them to read it aloud quickly. Can they do so without making a mistake? They could create lists of alliterative words and make up their own tongue-twisters.	**Reading AF5** Explain and comment on writers' uses of language, including grammatical and literary features at word and sentence level	211
7. Understanding and interpreting texts Explore how particular words are used, including words and expressions with similar meanings			
Tongue-twisters	**Tongue-twisters** encourages the use of adventurous word choices appropriate to the style of a poem. They draw on their knowledge and experience of tongue-twisters. This focuses on sounds that are difficult to pronounce one after the other. The children should first have opportunities to read some tongue-twisters and to identify the sounds that cause the problems. They should listen to the initial phonemes of words in the tongue-twisters and notice that repetition of identical phonemes is not difficult; it is slight differences that cause the problems: for example, d/dr/dw/j, g/gl/gr, r/l, p/pr/pl, k/c/qu, s/sh/ch/sl/sm/sn/st, t/tr/tw, w/r.	**All Writing AFs, especially:** **Writing AF1** Write imaginative, interesting and thoughtful texts **Writing AF2** Produce texts which are appropriate to task, reader and purpose **Writing AF7** Select appropriate and effective vocabulary	212
Riddles	**Riddles** encourages the use of adventurous word choices appropriate to the style of a poem. They draw on their knowledge and experience of riddles. The activity suggests a format for a riddle to spell the word star and to end with a clue to this word. The children should concentrate on writing clues for the letters rather than making the riddle rhyme. Here is an example of a completed riddle: My first is in sight but not in night My second is in tea but not in sea My third is in cat but not in cot My fourth is in rice but not in spice I twinkle and sparkle and make the night nice!		213
9. Creating and shaping texts Draw on knowledge and experience of texts in deciding and planning what and how to write			
Ask a silly question	**Ask a silly question** helps the children to make adventurous word choices appropriate to the style of a joke dialogue poem and supports them in writing question-and-answer jokes based on the dual meanings of words. They could also think up others of their own as they come across words that have two meanings.	**All Writing AFs, especially:** **Writing AF1** Write imaginative, interesting and thoughtful texts **Writing AF2** Produce texts which are appropriate to task, reader and purpose **Writing AF7** Select appropriate and effective vocabulary	214
Silly birthdays	**Silly birthdays** helps the children to make adventurous word choices appropriate to the style of a poem. They draw on their knowledge and experience of rhymes, as this provides a well-known alternative 'Happy birthday' song and a rhyme bank and structure to help them to write their own versions. They could take turns to sing their rhymes to the class.		215
9. Creating and shaping texts Make adventurous word and language choices appropriate to style and purpose of text			

Say it with letters

The alphabet people do not use words.
They say the names of letters.
• Read aloud what they are saying.

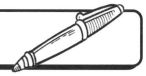
Use expression.

Sound as if you are trying to get your mum to do something.

Sound as if you are a teacher asking the class a question.

Sound as if you are trying to make your friend feel better.

Sound as if you are giving instructions.

NOW TRY THIS!

• Talk with a partner in 'letter talk'.
• Can you each tell what feeling the other is trying to show?

Teachers' note Use a puppet to introduce this. Explain and demonstrate that it cannot say words, only letters. Mime instructions or questions, saying only the names of letters of the alphabet at random or in groups. Can the children guess what you are saying? Let them practise speaking using only letters. Remind them how to use facial expressions, actions and tone of voice.

A Lesson for Every Day
Literacy
6-7 Years
© A&C Black

It's my house!

- **Talk to your partner about the story.**
- **Read the story aloud together.**

 Work with a partner.

NOW TRY THIS!

- **Record the story.**
- **Play it back.**
- **Record it again if you can improve it.**

Teachers' note Begin by covering all but the first four pictures. Discuss what is going on in the first three pictures and ask what happens in the fourth. Note that two additional characters are introduced. Ask what they wanted to do and what they might have said. Then ask what the first character replied. The children could predict what happens next.

A Lesson for Every Day
Literacy
6-7 Years
© A&C Black

Rhyme characters

On the way up the hill, Jack and Jill
met Humpty Dumpty and Little Bo Peep.
- **What did they say?**
- **Write in the speech bubbles.**
- **Act the scene.**

Work in a group of four.

NOW TRY THIS!
- **Talk about what might happen next.**
- **Act the story.**

Teachers' note Give each child a copy of this page. Remind the children of the nursery rhymes featured in this activity and ask them to identify the problem encountered by each character. Can the characters help one another (either practically or through giving advice)? Encourage the children to discuss what the characters might do as well as what they might say.

A Lesson for Every Day
Literacy
6-7 Years
© A&C Black

27

Elves

- **Work in a group of four.**
  Imagine you are these elves.
  What might you do? Write your ideas.
- **Act the story.**

matches

matches

Tea

Our ideas

NOW TRY THIS!

- **What if one of the people spots the elves?**
  Act the scene.

Teachers' note Give each group a copy of this page and ask them to appoint a scribe. Discuss the two settings within the house. Who lives above the floorboards and who lives below? Do they know about one another? Encourage the children to imagine they are the elves and talk (in role) about what is going on above the floorboards and how they might go there to collect things they need.

A Lesson for Every Day
Literacy
6–7 Years
© A&C Black

28

Mr Dozy's hat

- **Read the stories.**
- <u>**Underline**</u> **the words that have changed in the second story.**

Today it is raining. Mr Dozy wants to go to the shops.

He needs his hat. It is not on the hall table. Where is it?

Mr Dozy lifts the mat. He pulls out all the drawers.

He empties the bin. He searches the shed. He opens

the fridge. Now he is even looking in the bread bin.

Where is Mr Dozy's hat?

He is scratching his head. What is that on his head?

"Silly me," says Mr Dozy. His hat is on his head!

Yesterday it rained. Mr Dozy wanted to go to the shops.

He needed his hat. It was not on the hall table. Where was it?

Mr Dozy lifted the mat. He pulled out all the drawers.

He emptied the bin. He searched the shed. He opened

the fridge. Then he even looked in the bread bin.

Where was Mr Dozy's hat?

He scratched his head. What was that on his head?

"Silly me," said Mr Dozy. His hat was on his head!

NOW TRY THIS!

- **Think of other places where Mr Dozy could look for his hat.**
- **Tell a friend where he is looking today and where he looked yesterday.**

Teachers' note Read the first sentence of each passage aloud and ask the children if they can spot the difference. Ask them why one passage says it is raining and the other says it rained. Draw their attention to the words today and yesterday and introduce the term past for events that have already happened. During the plenary, ask the children to describe how words change for the past tense.

A Lesson for Every Day
Literacy
6-7 Years
© A&C Black

29

Mrs Forgetful

- **Read Mrs Forgetful's questions with a friend.**
- **Take turns to say the answers.**

Today I am walking to the shops.
Where did I walk yesterday?

Yesterday you walked to the park.

Today I am eating a peach.
What did I eat yesterday?

Today I am drinking milk.
What did I drink yesterday?

Today I am riding a horse.
What did I ride yesterday?

Today I am baking bread.
What did I bake yesterday?

NOW TRY THIS!

- **Tell your friend what you are doing today.**
- **Say what you did yesterday.**

30

Teachers' note The children should first have completed 'Mr Dozy's hat'. Remind them how words change to refer to past events. After they have completed the activity orally, invite feedback and write up their answers. Point out how words change to form the past tense: for some -**ed** is added, but for others there are different changes: for example, *eat/ate, drink/drank, ride/rode*.

A Lesson for Every Day
Literacy
6–7 Years
© A&C Black

Past endings

- **Read the words.**
- **Listen to the** ed **endings.**
- **Write them under the ending they sound like.**

lifted   shouted   talked   kicked

posted   dashed   mixed   tasted

counted   bounced   jumped   fainted

mend ed	**crash** ed

NOW TRY THIS!

- **Write two more** ed **words in each list.**
  Here are some clues: look, rush, trust, hunt.

Teachers' note The children should first have completed 'Mr Dozy's hat' and 'Mrs Forgetful'. Remind them how words change to refer to past events. Focus on those that take the **-ed** suffix. Display a completed copy of the past tense passage from page 29 on the whiteboard and ask the children to read the underlined words aloud. Ask them to repeat some of them, and demonstrate how to clap each syllable.

A Lesson for Every Day
Literacy
6-7 Years
© A&C Black

Program the robots

- **Read what the robots say.**
The word in the loop is wrong.
- **Say the correct word.**
- **Write it in the phoneme grid.**

Yesterday I cook some fish.

Yesterday I paint a picture.

Yesterday we want an ice cream.

Yesterday Mum pull up weeds in the garden.

Yesterday Dad mend the gate.

NOW TRY THIS!

You have been using the past tense .
- **Say these words in the past tense.**

search   play   plant   collect

- **Count the phonemes.**

Teachers' note Remind the children about the **-ed** suffix for forming the past tense. Use a phoneme grid to show how to form the past tense of examples from page 29, such as rained and wanted and draw attention to the number of phonemes in each **-ed** ending.

A Lesson for Every Day
Literacy
6-7 Years
© A&C Black

Base words with ed

- **Write the** $\boxed{\text{base words}}$ **in the** $\boxed{\text{past tense}}$.
- **Say the words.**

Base word

Past tense yesterday

blame ➡️

chase ➡️

wipe ➡️

hate ➡️

stroke ➡️

scrape ➡️

wade ➡️

squeeze ➡️

explode ➡️

NOW TRY THIS!

- **How did you change the base words?**
- **Tell a friend.**

Teachers' note Introduce the term base word. Remind the children about adding the -**ed** suffix to form the past tense of examples from page 29, such as scratched and lifted, then model other examples in which the base word ends with **e**, such as skate, like, wipe. Discuss how the base word changes and compare this with want, rain, snow and so on.

A Lesson for Every Day
Literacy
6–7 Years
© A&C Black

33

Copycats

- **Choose the correct** past tense **word.**
- **Write it in the gap.**
- **Read the** sentence **.**

copy	coped copied copyed	I _____ the letter.
hurry	hurryed hurred hurried	She _____ for the bus.
marry	married marred marryed	They were _____ last week.
tidy	tided tidyed tidied	Ben _____ his bedroom.
carry	carried carryed carred	Dad _____ the shopping.

NOW TRY THIS!

- **Write past tense sentences using words made from these.**

  worry   scurry   pity

Teachers' note Remind the children about adding the -**ed** suffix to form the past tense of examples from page 29, such as *rained* and *wanted*, then model other examples in which the base word ends with **y**, such as *empty, bury, bully*. Discuss how the base word changes before -**ed** is added.

A Lesson for Every Day
Literacy
6-7 Years
© A&C Black

Mixed doubles

- **Read the sentences.**
- **Tell a friend how the** ⟨base words⟩ **change.**

Today I ⟨hop⟩ along the path.

Yesterday I <u>hopped</u> along the path.

- **Change these base words to the past tense.**

chop_____

   rob_____

clap_____

pat_____

drop_____

trip_____

drum_____

chat_____

trot_____

knit_____

- **Write three words that follow the same rule as the others on this page.**

Teachers' note Remind the children about adding the **-ed** suffix to form the past tense of examples from page 29. Model other examples in which the base word ends with a consonant that must be doubled to preserve a vowel or consonant phoneme: for example, *bat, hug, slip, step, wag*. Discuss how the word changes before **-ed** is added.

A Lesson for Every Day
Literacy
6-7 Years
© A&C Black

Match and sort: ed

play	played	point	pointed
clasp	clasped	search	searched
cheat	cheated	squash	squashed
ferry	ferried	poke	poked
ache	ached	use	used
bully	bullied	beg	begged
sob	sobbed	drip	dripped
clip	clipped	slap	slapped

Teachers' note Ask the children what they have learned about adding **-ed** to base words to form the past tense. They could give examples from previous pages. After cutting out the cards they could play 'Matching pairs' or 'Find your partner' (see Notes on the activities, page 7).

A Lesson for Every Day
Literacy
6–7 Years
© A&C Black

Sad to say

Story title

_____

- **Draw and name the characters .**
- **Write in their speech bubbles.**

Main character

[ ]

I was sad because . _____

_____

_____

_____

Name _____

Another character

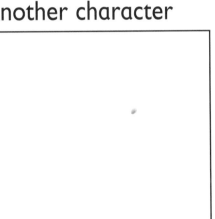

This is how I helped.

_____

_____

_____

_____

Name _____

NOW TRY THIS!

- **Tell the story with a friend.**
- **Show how the characters feel.**

Teachers' note Use this to help the children to focus on the response of a story character to a problem, mishap or other major event in a story and how another character interacts with him or her. Reread parts of the story and ask how the character felt. Ask the children what happened to make him or her feel better, who helped, and how.

A Lesson for Every Day
Literacy
6-7 Years
© A&C Black

Amazing Grace

Grace loves stories.
She acts them out.
There is going to be a
pantomime at school.
Grace wants to be Peter Pan.
This is what some children say:

Amazing Grace is a story by Mary Hoffman.

You can't. Peter Pan's a boy.

Raj

You can't. Peter Pan isn't black.

Natalie

- **Write what Grace said.**

- **What will Grace do?**
  Will she be Peter Pan? How?
- **Tell the story.**

Teachers' note This is based on *Amazing Grace* by Mary Hoffman (Frances Lincoln). Ask the children to describe Grace; draw out what she is like, including her interest in, and talent for, acting. You could also talk about what made her sad and who helped.

A Lesson for Every Day
Literacy
6-7 Years
© A&C Black

Leon and Bob story map

Leon and Bob is a story by Simon James.

• Retell the story using the pictures.

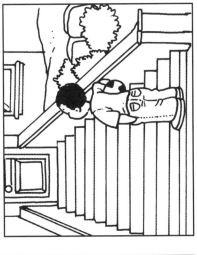

NOW TRY THIS!

• How did Leon change?

• Tell a friend what was different about Leon.

Teachers' note This is based on *Leon and Bob* by Simon James. The children can use the story map to help them to retell the story in their own words. Afterwards, encourage them to think about Leon's feelings at each stage and to tell the story in a way which expresses these.

A Lesson for Every Day
Literacy
6-7 Years
© **A&C Black**

Feelings

- **How do the characters** feel **?**
- **Write in the boxes.**

"Over here!" screamed Runa.

[ ]

"We missed it," sighed Jan.

[ ]

"We missed it," growled Lee.

[ ]

Word-bank

angry

disappointed

excited

frightened

happy

pleased

"What a goal!" exclaimed Sam.

[ ]

"Look at that!" whispered Mick, trembling.

[ ]

"Look at that!" smiled Dan.

[ ]

NOW TRY THIS!

- **Underline the words that give you a clue to how the characters feel.**

Teachers' note After reading a section of a story in which characters' feelings are communicated through what they say, and how, ask the children how the character felt and how they could tell. Focus on words which express how they speak, as well as discussing what they say and how they have changed.

A Lesson for Every Day
Literacy
6-7 Years
© A&C Black

Salim's new bike

• **Write the next part of the story.**

Salim lifted his right leg over the crossbar of his new bike. He tried to sit on the shiny black saddle but it was just a bit too high. His eyes shone as he gripped the handles. The handles came up on stalks from the bright yellow frame.

Tomorrow his dad was going to take him to the park to ride it. He picked up a big old curtain and spread the heavy red cloth over his bike. Then he closed the door of the shed and clicked the padlock. He had to keep it safe.

Something happens

Make readers want to read on.

_____

_____

_____

_____

_____

_____

_____

_____

NOW TRY THIS!

• **Write the opening and the ending of the story.**

Teachers' note Read the passage with the children and ask them how Salim feels. What does the story suggest that might worry him? Ask them what might happen. Draw out that the mention of locking the shed to keep the bike safe helps to prepare the next part of the story (something might happen to the bike).

A Lesson for Every Day
Literacy
6–7 Years
© A&C Black

The competition

- Plan a story about a competition.
- Draw and write your ideas.

Main character **Opening** Setting

Something happens

It is sorted out

Ending

NOW TRY THIS!

- Write some notes about each part of the story.

Teachers' note Ask the children about competitions they have entered – how they felt after they had entered and were waiting for the results and what they did during this time. Discuss anything that could have gone wrong. How could this be put right?

A Lesson for Every Day
Literacy
6-7 Years
© A&C Black

A special treat: 1

- **Write notes on the story plan.**

Simon
Age 7

Loves playing football

Supports team

Watches them on TV

Has never been to live match

What he is like _____

_____

Family, friends _____

_____

Where he plays _____

_____

Playing and watching football _____

_____

Gets 2 tickets for match

Excited

Can't wait

How he gets tickets _____

_____

_____

The match _____

Teams _____

_____

When _____

Where _____

_____

NOW TRY THIS!

- **Write the first sentence of each part of the story.**

| Beginning | | What happens |

Teachers' note Tell the children about Simon, the boy featured in this activity, and ask them what they think he might like as a special treat. Let them read about Simon's special treat. They fill in the details about Simon and begin telling a story about the treat and who arranged it for him. Continued on 'A special treat: 2'.

A Lesson for Every Day
Literacy
6–7 Years
© A&C Black

43

A special treat: 2

• **Write notes on the story plan.**

Can't wait for big day

Tells friends

Dreams about match

What Simon does _____

_____

What they say and do _____

_____

_____

His dreams _____

_____

_____

The problem _____

_____

_____

A problem

Shock

Will miss match

What Simon says and does _____

_____

_____

What will happen _____

_____

_____

NOW TRY THIS!

• **Write two sentences to start each part of the story.**

| Simon can't wait | Problem |

Teachers' note See page 'A special treat: 1'. Invite the children to continue the story. Ask them how Simon feels about the special treat and how his friends might feel when he tells them. They could talk about how he dreams of the big day, and what might happen. Then ask them what might go wrong. What could spoil it? Continued on 'A special treat: 3'.

A Lesson for Every Day
Literacy
6-7 Years
© **A&C Black**

A special treat: 3

• **Write notes on the story plan.**

Solution

Something happens to help

What happens _____

_____

_____

_____

How it helps _____

_____

_____

_____

Ending

Surprise _____

_____

_____

Ending _____

_____

_____

What might happen afterwards _____

_____

NOW TRY THIS!

• **Write two sentences to start each part of the story.**

| solution | ending |

Teachers' note See 'A special treat: 1 and 2'. Invite volunteers to talk about their stories so far. Why did events happen; focus on how one event leads on to another. Ask the children what problem Simon has and what could happen in their stories to solve it. They should consider the end of the story and the ideas they have about what might happen after that (in another story).

A Lesson for Every Day
Literacy
6-7 Years
© A&C Black

Chosen

This story character has been chosen for something special.
- Write questions to ask her.
- Write the answers with a friend.

Questions   Answers

What is going to happen?

NOW TRY THIS!
- Use the questions and
  answers to help you to plan
  a story.

Teachers' note Tell the children that the story character has been chosen for something special: for example, to do something, to go somewhere or to meet someone. What questions would they would like to ask her to find out more about this?

A Lesson for Every Day
Literacy
6–7 Years
© A&C Black

Cross the road

- **Play with a partner.**
- **Take turns to colour a footprint to make a sentence.**
- **Join these footprints. The first to cross the road wins.**

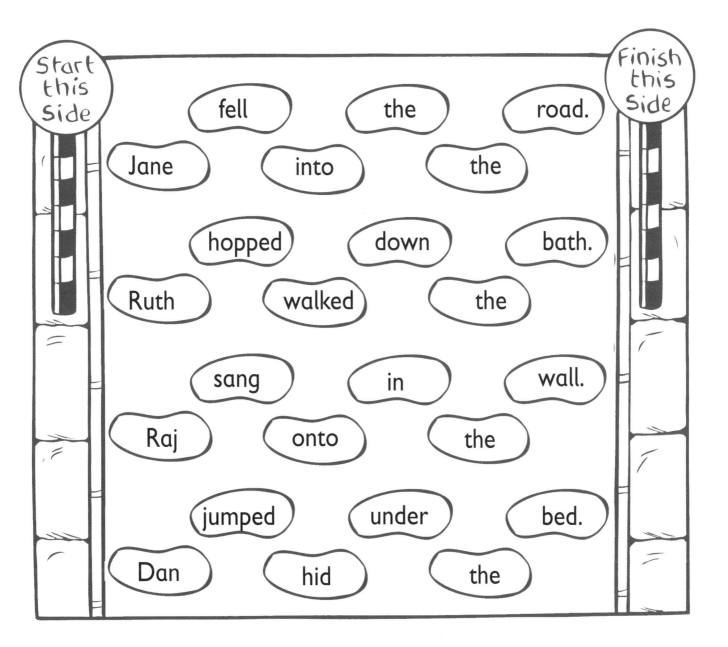

Start this Side

Finish this Side

fell   the   road.

Jane   into   the

hopped   down   bath.

Ruth   walked   the

sang   in   wall.

Raj   onto   the

jumped   under   bed.

Dan   hid   the

NOW TRY THIS!

- **Copy two of your sentences.**
- **Add one or two words to make them longer.**

Teachers' note Model how to complete a sentence: start with the person the sentence is about (for example, Jane) and then choose a word for what she did. Ask what could come next. It is useful to think aloud and explain why *fell* or *hopped* cannot come next, using the + *road* or the + *bath* as examples: Jane could not fall or hop anything but she could fall *into* the bath or *down* the road.

A Lesson for Every Day
Literacy
6-7 Years
© A&C Black

Sentence wall

The words must make sentences.

- Play with a partner. Take turns to colour a brick.
The first to cross the wall with a sentence wins.

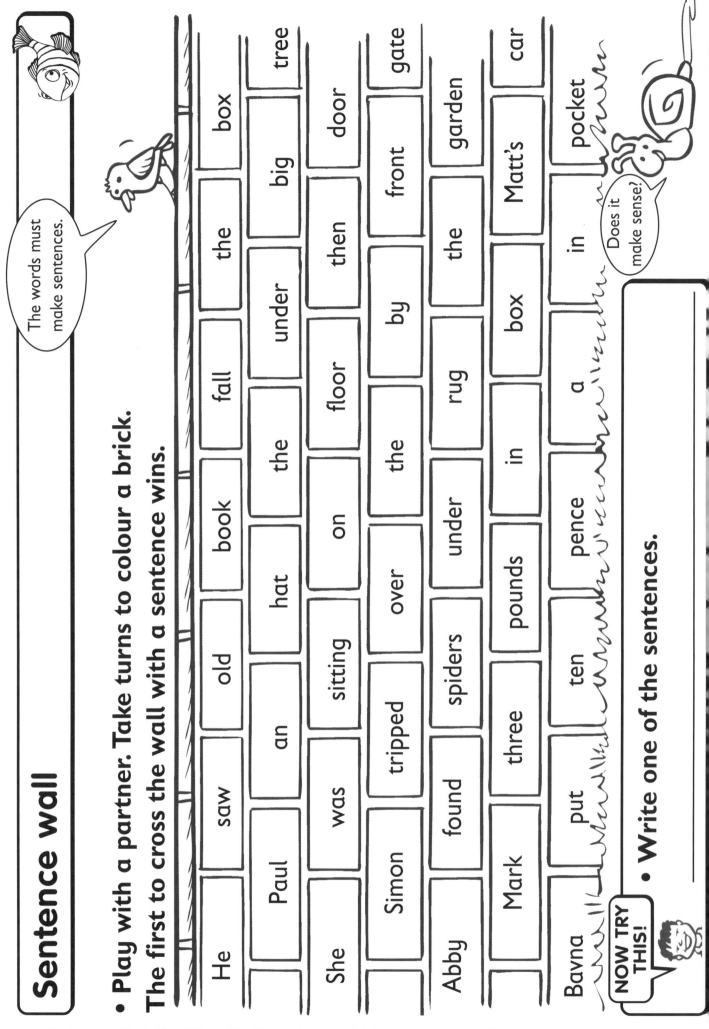

He	saw	old	book	the	fall	the	big	box
Paul		an	hat		under	then		tree
She	was	sitting	on	over	the	floor	by	door
Simon		tripped				the		gate
Abby	found	spiders	under	rug	in	the		garden
Mark	three	pounds	in	box	Matt's		front
Bavna	put	ten	pence	a	in		car
							Matt's	pocket

Does it make sense?

NOW TRY THIS!

- Write one of the sentences.

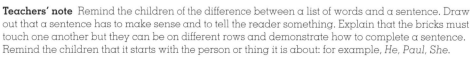

Teachers' note Remind the children of the difference between a list of words and a sentence. Draw out that a sentence has to make sense and to tell the reader something. Explain that the bricks must touch one another but they can be on different rows and demonstrate how to complete a sentence. Remind the children that it starts with the person or thing it is about: for example, *He, Paul, She*.

A Lesson for Every Day
Literacy
6–7 Years
© A&C Black

48

Where words

There are a lot of words for ⬚where⬚. **Here are some of them.**

Where word-bank

across	along	by	down	in	near
next to	on	over	under	up	

- **Write** ⬚where⬚ **words in the gaps.**

1 Alex hid _____ the duvet.

2 Sunita fell _____ the stairs.

3 When it was safe we walked _____ the road.

4 There was no one _____ the house.

5 We had to go _____ a steep hill.

6 There was a car park _____ the shops.

7 He sang as he walked _____ the road.

8 Roop's house is _____ mine.

9 There were two mugs _____ the table.

10 The school is _____ a park.

NOW TRY THIS!

- **Write three sentences about a walk.**
- **Use as many** ⬚where⬚ **words as you can.**

Teachers' note Review the children's previous learning about the different parts of a sentence by reminding them of the questions they were asked: Who? What? When? Where? Read the words in the word-bank and draw out that they can be used in sentences to say where something happened.

A Lesson for Every Day
Literacy
6-7 Years
© A&C Black

Now
I am talking
or
I talk

Then
I was talking
or
I talked

• **Fill in the gaps.**

Now	Then
I am walking. I walk.	I was _____. I _____.
I am _____. I _____.	I was _____. I sang.
I am _____. I _____.	I was sitting. I _____.
I am playing. I _____.	I was _____. I _____.
I am _____. I eat.	I was _____. I ate.

NOW TRY THIS!

• **Write** **now** **and** **then** **sentences using these words:**
    jump   ride

Teachers' note Explain that we change the words for what we do depending on whether we are doing it now or have already done it. Demonstrate how to complete the first question and give examples of sentences in which the verbs are used: for example, *I am walking to school now, I walk to school every day, I was walking to school when I met my friend, I walked to school this morning.*

A Lesson for Every Day
Literacy
6–7 Years
© A&C Black

Story mix

- **What happens when characters from different stories meet?**
- **Write your ideas on the notepad.**
- **Write in the speech bubbles.**

 Work with a partner.

Snow White's stepmother

Giant from 'Jack and the Beanstalk'

A Lesson for Every Day
Literacy
6-7 Years
© A&C Black

 **NOW TRY THIS!**

- **Tell the story.**

Teachers' note The children should first have read (or listened to) the story of *Snow White and the Seven Dwarfs* and *Jack and the Beanstalk*. They could re-tell the stories. Imagine that Snow White's stepmother met the Giant. How would these characters get on and how might they change one another's stories? In the activity, the children could focus on one of the stories.

Story listener

- **Listen to someone reading a story.**
- **Write about it on the notepad.**
- **Fill in the faces.**
- **Write on the lines.**

Title _____

Author _____

How well could you hear the story?	How well did the reader look at the audience?
How well did the reader use his or her face and actions?	How well did the reader change his or her voice for different characters?
Give an example	Give an example
_____ _____ _____ _____	_____ _____ _____ _____

NOW TRY THIS!

- **What was the best part of the story reading?**
- **What did you like about this part?**

Teachers' note Ask a volunteer who is a confident reader to read a story to the class (or read it yourself). The audience can then evaluate the reading and use the examples to justify their comments.

A Lesson for Every Day
Literacy
6-7 Years
© A&C Black

The best dishcloth: 1

Asma, Jason, Leah and Karl have been testing dishcloths.

- **Listen to what they did.**

We tested four cloths: a piece of towelling, a J-cloth, a 'super absorbent' cloth and a cotton dishcloth.

Asma

We cut a small piece from each cloth. The pieces were the same size.

Jason

We dropped spoonfuls of water onto each cloth. We stopped when it wouldn't soak up any more water.

Leah

We counted the spoonfuls.

Karl

- **Here are the children's results:**

Cloth	Number of spoonfuls of water it soaked up
Towelling	10
J-cloth	4
Super-absorbent cloth	16
Cotton dishcloth	8

NOW TRY THIS!

- **What else do you want to know about the test?**
- **Ask your teacher a question.**
- **Write the question and the answer.**

Think what you need to know to do the same test.

Teachers' note You could ask four children to read the words in the speech bubbles and others to read the chart while another group listens. They could then tell a different group about it, and so on.

A Lesson for Every Day
Literacy
6-7 Years
© A&C Black

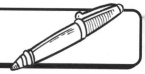

- **Read the sentences about what the dishcloth test showed.**
- **Write** | true | **or** | false | **in the boxes.**

The super-absorbent cloth was the strongest.

The towelling cloth was the best for mopping up spilt drinks.

The J-cloth was the best for drying things.

The cotton dishcloth soaked up the most water.

The super-absorbent cloth had the nicest colour.

The super-absorbent cloth was the best for mopping up spills.

NOW TRY THIS!

- **Write another sentence about the test.**
- **Give it to a partner to write** | true | **or** | false |.

Teachers' note Remind the children of 'good listening'. Re-read the information on 'The best dishcloth: 1' to them and ask them to answer the questions about it.

A Lesson for Every Day
Literacy
6-7 Years
© A&C Black

54

- **Listen to this story.**
- **Then read it again with your group.**

The king of Ayodhya was growing old. He said that his son Rama should be the next king.

But Queen Kaykai was the mother of the king's second son, Bharata. She remembered when she had encouraged the king when he was losing a battle. He went out and won. He told her that he would grant her whatever she wished. She had never asked for anything. Now she would.

"I now want you to grant my wish," she said to the king. "Banish Rama from the kingdom. My son Bharata will be the next king."

The king could not go back on his word, and so Rama and his wife Sita were sent off into the forest. Rama went hunting for food. He drew a magic circle around Sita. "Stay there and you will be safe," he said.

Ravana, the king of the demons, was watching. He sent a young deer which had been hurt. Sita saw it and stepped out of the circle to help it. Ravana pounced on her and carried her off to his palace on the island of Lanka.

When Rama came back, he guessed what had happened. He called on his friend, the king of the monkeys. All the monkeys of India came to help. They linked their arms and tails and made a bridge across the sea to Lanka. Rama went with them. He killed Ravana the demon with an arrow from his golden bow. Rama and the monkeys rushed in and rescued Sita. They marched back to Ayodhya. The people were so happy that they put little lights called divas in their windows.

Teachers' note Use this with 'Rama and Sita: 2'. Split the class into groups of four and give each group a copy of this page. Read the story to the class, then allow time for the children to read it again in their groups before making the stick puppets. These can also be used as 'shadow puppets': shine a bright torch, slide projector or overhead projector to project shadows onto a screen made from white paper or cloth.

A Lesson for Every Day
Literacy
6-7 Years
© A&C Black

Rama and Sita: 2

- **Cut out the puppets.**
  Glue them onto lollipop sticks
- **Act part of the story of Rama and Sita.**

Work in a group of four.

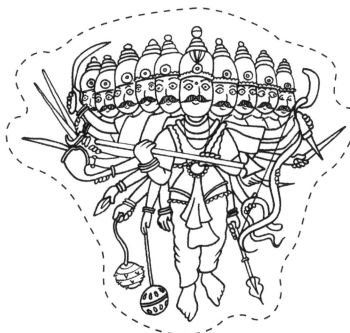

Sita

Rama

The demon Ravana

The monkey king

Teachers' note Use this with 'Rama and Sita: 1'. Copy the page onto card, enlarging it to A3 if you wish. Each group needs one copy of the sheet and four lollipop sticks. The group should chose part of the story and enact it using a puppet each, speaking in role. Encourage them to use their voices to express feelings such as sadness, happiness, fear and determination. Invite groups to perform to the class.

A Lesson for Every Day
Literacy
6–7 Years
© A&C Black

Name clapping

- **Read the names.**
- **Clap for each beat.**
- **Write the number of claps.**

Anna → An | na

Andrew ○

Salim ○

James ○

Christopher ○

Angela ○

Alice ○

Rosemary ○

Benjamin ○

Sita ○

Max ○

Amy ○

Elizabeth ○

NOW TRY THIS!

- **Clap the name of a fairytale character for a friend to guess.**
- **Write the name.**

Teachers' note Begin by clapping the syllables of the children's names as you say them. Invite the children to join in. Then clap a name but do not say it. Ask the children to hold up their hand if it could be their name.

A Lesson for Every Day
Literacy
6-7 Years
© A&C Black

 ditch

 caught

 palm

 word

 naughty

 almond

 fetch

 worm

 daughter

 world

 calf

 patch

 work

 half

 clutch

 taught

Teachers' note Use this with 'Happy families: 2'. The children could cut out the cards and sort them into groups of four words with similar spelling patterns. The cards can also be used for a game of 'Happy Families' for a group of four: show the children how to deal four cards to each of their group and place the rest face down in a pile on the table. Continued on page 59.

A Lesson for Every Day
Literacy
6-7 Years
© **A&C Black**

Happy families: 2

pear

nature

snowman

school

chemist

rainbow

bear

future

pillow

wear

mixture

echo

ache

picture

grow

heard

Teachers' note Tell the children the object of the game: to collect a family of four words with similar spellings. If they already have a set of four they can 'declare' this on their turn. The player to the dealer's left is first to play. He or she can 'declare' or take a card unseen from the next player and put one face down at the bottom of the pile on the table in return. The first to 'declare' wins.

A Lesson for Every Day
Literacy
6-7 Years
© **A&C Black**

59

Long words: 1

- **Clap and count.**
- **Draw the lines.**
- **Write the letters.**

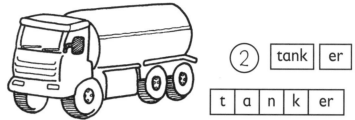

② | tank | er |

| t | a | n | k | er |

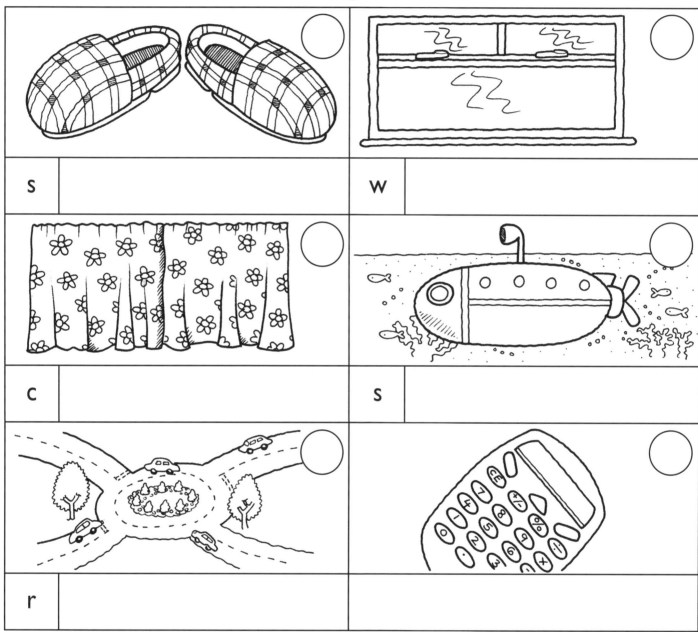

s		w	
c		s	
r			

NOW TRY THIS!

- **Write a word for a small black creature with too many legs to count.**

Teachers' note Use this page to help the children to tackle the spelling of longer words. They should first have had experience of clapping the syllables of familiar words such as their names. Use the completed example to show them how to clap and count the syllables of tanker and then to count the phonemes and draw a phoneme frame on which to write the word.

A Lesson for Every Day
Literacy
6–7 Years
© A&C Black

Long words: 2

- **Clap and count.**
- **Draw the lines.**
- **Write the letters.**

②	coff	ee

c	o	ff	ee

l

s

c

l

NOW TRY THIS!

- **Write two words for fruits that are like small oranges.**

Teachers' note Use this page to help the children to tackle the spelling of longer words. They should first have had experience of clapping the syllables of familiar words such as their names. Use the completed example to show them how to clap and count the syllables of coffee and then to count the phonemes and draw a phoneme frame on which to write the word.

A Lesson for Every Day
Literacy
6-7 Years
© A&C Black

In short

• **Write these the short way. Remember the apostrophe.**

Examples:

Who's there?

Who is there?

It's Grandma.

It is Grandma.

What is the time, Mr Wolf?

It is six o'clock.

Where is Sam?

He is in the shed.

How is May?

She is very well.

NOW TRY THIS!

• **Write sentences using their short forms.**

| we shall | I would | I did not |

Teachers' note Use examples from stories the children have read to introduce contractions. Model changing example sentences by saying the entire words: for instance, *I'm going to eat you/I am going to eat you*. You could also speak to the children without using contractions and ask them what sounds unusual. Help them to identify the words that are usually contracted.

A Lesson for Every Day
Literacy
6-7 Years
© A&C Black

These words have been split up for you to clap.

- **Clap the words.**
- **Sound the** | phonemes | **in each part.**
- **Read the words.**

| h | o | s | | p | i | | t | a | l | → | hospital |

| c | e | n | | t | i | | p | e | d | e | → | centipede |

| g | a | | l | a | x | y | → | galaxy |

| d | a | ff | | o | | d | i | l | → | daffodil |

| c | r | o | c | | o | | d | i | l | e | → | crocodile |

NOW TRY THIS!

- **Read these long words with a friend.**

| telephone | | caretaker | | electric |

Teachers' note Use this page to help the children to read longer words. They should first have had experience of clapping the syllables of familiar words such as their names. Model how to split a word into syllables by writing it on card and then cutting it into syllables. The phonemes in each syllable can then be separated by drawing lines between them.

A Lesson for Every Day
Literacy
6-7 Years
© A&C Black

Syllables and phonemes: 2

These words have been split up for you to clap.

- **Clap the words.**
- **Sound the** | phonemes | **in each part.**
- **Fill the gaps.**
- **Read the words.**

| e | l | | ph | a | n | t | ➞ elephant

| t | e | l | | s | c | o | p | e | ➞ telescope

| m | i | c | | | w | a | v | e | ➞ microwave

| | | | p | u | t | e | r | ➞ computer

| e | n | v | e | l | | | | ➞ envelope

| | | p | er | | | k | e | t | ➞ supermarket

NOW TRY THIS!

- **Read these long words with a friend.**

| magnetic | | caterpillar | | hippopotamus |

Teachers' note Use this page to help the children to read longer words. They should first have had experience of clapping the syllables of familiar words such as their names. Model how to split a word into syllables by writing it on card and then cutting it into syllables. The phonemes in each syllable can then be separated by drawing lines between them.

A Lesson for Every Day
Literacy
6–7 Years
© A&C Black

What if...?

The King and Queen invited all the fairies to see the baby.

- What if the baby had been a boy?
- Write what the good fairies would have said.
- Write what the bad fairy would have said.

THE SLEEPING BEAUTY

NOW TRY THIS!

- What might happen next?
- Talk to a friend about the story.

Teachers' note This is based on the fairytale *The Sleeping Beauty*. Read the beginning of the story and use this page to help the children to retell the story so far and to imagine what might have happened if the baby had been a boy.

A Lesson for Every Day
Literacy
6-7 Years
© A&C Black

Character change

- **What was Red Riding Hood like in the two stories?**

Little Red Riding Hood

What she was like

_____

_____

How I can tell

_____

_____

_____

The True Story of Little Red Riding Hood

What she was like

_____

_____

How I can tell

_____

_____

_____

NOW TRY THIS!

- **What was the Wolf like in the two stories? How can you tell?**

Teachers' note The children first need to have read the traditional tale _Little Red Riding Hood_. Discuss each story: ask the children what Red Riding Hood was like and how they can tell. They should support what they say with examples from the stories.

A Lesson for Every Day
Literacy
6–7 Years
© A&C Black

Good wolf and bad wolf on screen

- **Sort the sounds and pictures.**

Good wolf

Bad wolf

thunder and lightning

a bubbling stream

a roll of drums

a cheerful pipe

GRRRR

It's a hap-hap-happy day...

NOW TRY THIS!

- **List your ideas for showing the wolves on screen.**

| background | sounds | objects |

Teachers' note The children need to look at pictures (still or animated) of story characters and to notice how the good and evil characters are depicted. Can they tell from a picture whether a character is good or evil? How? Focus on the appearance and the background or screen effects and, where relevant, any accompanying sounds.

A Lesson for Every Day
Literacy
6-7 Years
© A&C Black

The three Bully Goats Gruff

- **Write what the characters said.**

Old stories said that the three billy goats just wanted some sweet fresh grass.

Keep him talking. I'll come and butt him. Ha, ha, ha!

Guzzler Gruff

Grabber Gruff

Then I'll toss him with my horns.

Greedy Gruff

Oh, no! Not that gang of goats.

This is the true story of the gang of Bully Goats.
They bullied a poor Troll just because he was ugly.

NOW TRY THIS!

How is this story different from the old one?
- **Talk to a friend about it.**

Teachers' note The children should first read the traditional story *The Three Billy Goats Gruff*. Ask them to look at the picture and introduction on this page. What might the goats be saying? What do their new names say about them? What do the children think they are like, and why? See also 'The bullied Troll', page 69.

A Lesson for Every Day
Literacy
6-7 Years
© A&C Black

The bullied Troll

What can the Troll do about the bullying?

- **Write notes.**
- **Use your notes to help you to write a letter to the Troll.**

Work with a group.

Notes

_____

_____

_____

_____

_____

Dear Troll

_____

_____

_____

_____

_____

_____

_____

_____

_____

With best wishes from

_____

Teachers' note The children should have completed 'The three Bully Goats Gruff' and have told/ written the opening of their story about the three Bully Goats. How might the Troll feel? What should he do? The children could discuss how the Troll could find help and what advice they would give him before they write these ideas in a letter to him. See also 'The Troll's diary', page 70.

A Lesson for Every Day
Literacy
6-7 Years
© A&C Black

69

The Troll's diary

The Troll kept a diary of what the Bully Goats did.
• Fill in the Troll's diary.

Write notes.

Date	What happened	What I did

NOW TRY THIS!

• **Write notes about what the Bully Goats said to one another.**

Teachers' note The children should first have completed 'The three Bully Goats Gruff' and 'The bullied Troll'. Discuss the use of a diary for someone to record each time he or she is bullied and how this is useful. The children can then think up incidents in which the Bully Goats bully the Troll. They should write the diary as if they are the Troll (using *I* and *me*). See also 'The Troll's solution', page 71.

A Lesson for Every Day
Literacy
6-7 Years
© A&C Black

70

The Troll's solution

How did the Troll solve the problem
of the Bully Goats?
• **Write notes.**

 What shall
I do?

Other characters

How they helped

_____

_____

_____

_____

_____

_____

_____

What happened

_____

_____

_____

_____

Ending

_____

_____

NOW TRY THIS!

• **Use your notes to help you to write
the story.**

Teachers' note The children should first complete pages 'The three Bully Goats Gruff', 'The bullied
Troll' and 'The Troll's diary'. Invite volunteers to tell their stories so far and to suggest how the Troll might
solve his problem. They should introduce characters from other traditional tales and say how they
might help. Give them time to talk about their stories or to enact them with a group before they write.

A Lesson for Every Day
Literacy
6-7 Years
© A&C Black

Sentence maker

- **Roll the dice.**
- **Move your counter.**
- **Write the words you land on.**

Can you make a sentence?

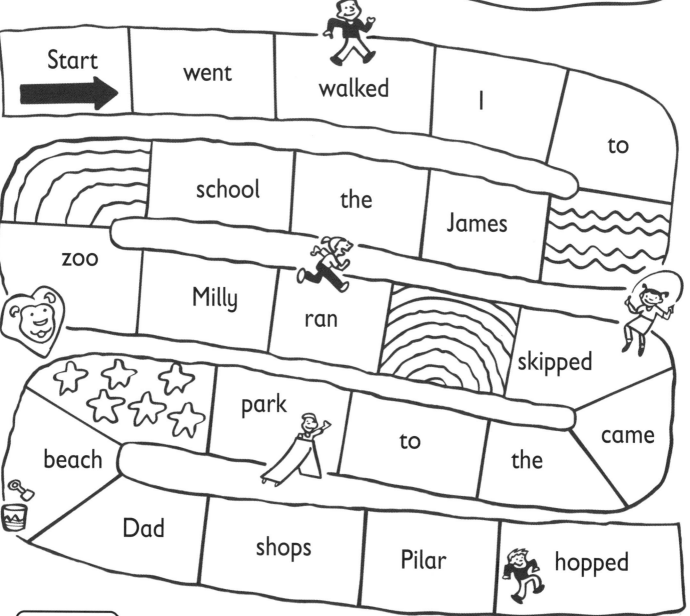

Start

went

walked

I

to

school

the

James

zoo

Milly

ran

skipped

park

to

the

came

beach

Dad

shops

Pilar

hopped

NOW TRY THIS!

- **Use the words on the game board to write two sentences.**

72 **Teachers' note** Ask children to work in groups of four. Provide pencils or pens and small pieces of paper for them all to record the words they land on. Encourage them to read the words they have written after each throw and make a sentence with them. After the next throw they could add a word to an existing sentence, begin a new one or move a word from one sentence to another.

A Lesson for Every Day
Literacy
6-7 Years
© A&C Black

Link up

• **Join three large owls to make sentences.**

Who?

two boys

an old woman

ten girls

Mr Jones

my mum

What?

got lost

went to town

lost a hat

sang a song

slid down the slide

When?

last night.

at bedtime.

after tea.

this morning.

yesterday.

NOW TRY THIS!

• **Write three other sentences which answer these questions.**

Who?   What?   When?

Teachers' note Point out that the owls should be linked down, not across, the page. Draw attention to the questions *Who?*, *What?* and *When?* Draw out that each sentence begins with the person or thing it is about. Next come some words to say *what* he, she or it did (and sometimes *where*). Finally come some words to say *when* it happened. Model an example.

A Lesson for Every Day
Literacy
6–7 Years
© A&C Black

Surprising endings: 1

- ## Read a story to a partner.
- ## Your partner makes up a surprising ending.

Bob the burglar

"I am no good at anything," said Bob. "I'll never get a job. I think I'll be a burglar."

One night Bob went to look for a house to break into. He tried a few doors to see if they were locked. Then he saw a house with an open window. All the lights were off. No one was home. Bob climbed through the window. He found lots of parcels wrapped in bright paper. "Presents. Brilliant! It's as good as a birthday," he said, and he pushed all the presents into his burglar sack. Bob couldn't wait to get home to open the presents.

Flora the flower girl

There was once a girl named Flora. She drew flowers. Lots of them – daffodils, lupins, poppies, lilies, pansies, hollyhocks, sunflowers. She drew every kind of flower. She filled her school books with flowers – all down the sides of her work, in between the words – everywhere. Her teacher was very cross.

"This must stop!" he said. "From now on you may draw only one flower in your books each day. No more."

So the next day Flora drew one beautiful petunia in her maths book. There was an addition on every petal and a subtraction on every leaf. Then it was time for a history lesson. She wanted to draw a geranium but she would be in trouble. She wanted to draw a delphinium and a daisy and a harebell... and a crocus and a hyacinth...

NOW TRY THIS!

- ## Change the ending of a fairytale.
- ## Make it surprising.

Teachers' note Different groups of children could work on different stories (cut out the stories on this page and 'Surprising endings: 2'), with each pair presenting their finished story to the group (see also 'My surprising ending').

A Lesson for Every Day
Literacy
6-7 Years
© A&C Black

Surprising endings: 2

- **Read a story to a partner.**
- **Your partner makes up a surprising ending.**

Sausages

There was once a boy who was afraid of sausages. Every time there were sausages for lunch he ran home from school. He crossed the road to get away from hot dog stalls. Once day his dad said, "Saveloy, you are seven years old. You must stop being such a coward."

"Right. I'm not going to be a coward," said Saveloy.

The next day, on the way to school, what should he see in the gutter but a lost sausage? So he jumped on it. He stamped. He shouted. He squashed the sausage.

That day what should it be for lunch? Yes, sausages – bangers and mash.

Cave boy

Many years ago when the land was covered in forests and people lived in caves, a boy shivered in his cave bedroom. He huddled inside his bearskin rug.

One day he said to his family, "I am fed up with being cold. I am fed up with sleeping on a slab of rock. I am fed up with hunting sabre-toothed tigers. I am fed up with trapping woolly mammoths. I am fed up with going out in the cold and rain to catch fish."

His father said, "Well, don't just complain. Do something about it!"

"I will," shouted the boy angrily.

NOW TRY THIS!

- **Change the ending of a fairytale.**
- **Make it surprising.**

Teachers' note Different groups of children could work on different stories (cut out the stories on this page and 'Surprising endings: 1'), with each pair presenting their finished story to the group (see also 'My surprising ending').

A Lesson for Every Day
Literacy
6-7 Years
© A&C Black

My surprising ending

- **Listen to the beginning of a story.**
- **Talk to a partner about what might happen next.**
- **Make up a surprising ending.**

Write notes.

Title _____

Main character

_____
_____
_____

What has happened so far

_____
_____
_____

What the character might do

_____
_____
_____
_____
_____
_____
_____

Surprise ending

NOW TRY THIS!

- **Use your notes to help you to tell the story.**

Teachers' note Use this sheet with pages 'Surprising endings: 1 and 2'. Ask the children to listen carefully to the story their friend reads and to notice clues about what might happen. Encourage them to recap and then to think of different possibilities. Can they come up with one they think will surprise their audience?

A Lesson for Every Day
Literacy
6–7 Years
© A&C Black

Charity choice: 1

- **Work in pairs.**
- **Find out about a charity.**
- **Write notes on the collection bucket.**

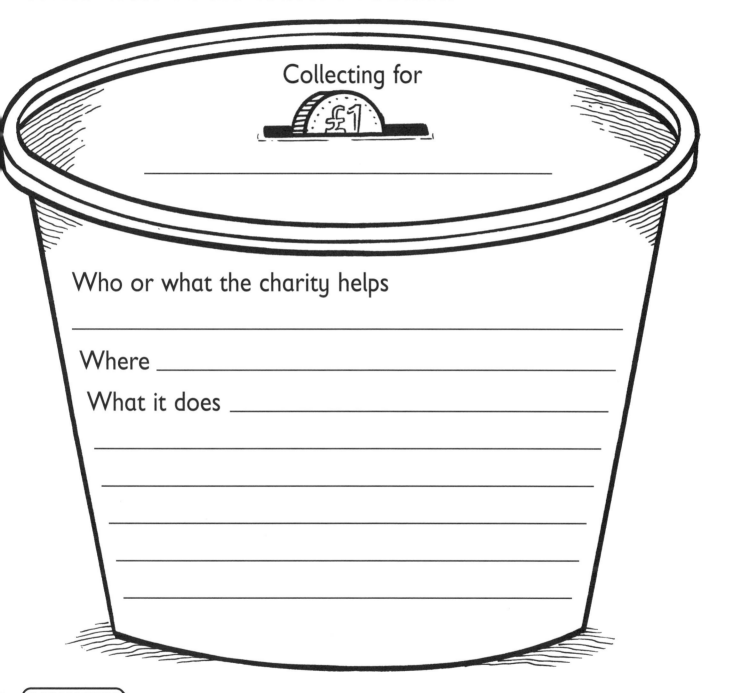

Collecting for

_____

Who or what the charity helps

_____

Where _____

What it does _____

_____

_____

_____

_____

_____

NOW TRY THIS!

- **List the most important facts about the charity.**

Teachers' note The children could be given the task of choosing a charity for the class to support: this involves finding out about the charity so that they can tell others, and then discussing with their group which one to support (see 'Charity choice: 2').

A Lesson for Every Day
Literacy
6-7 Years
© A&C Black

Charity choice: 2

- **Work in a group.**
- **Discuss which charity you would like to help.**
- **Write your choice.**
- **Write three reasons to help the charity.**

Charity
Why we want to help it
1
2
3

NOW TRY THIS!

- **Take a class vote on which charity to help.**

Teachers' note The children should first have completed 'Charity choice: 1'. Each pair could speak to the class or group about a charity. They should listen carefully to each presentation to find out as much as possible about the charity. Work in groups to choose one charity to support, justifying their choice to convince the rest of the class.

A Lesson for Every Day
Literacy
6-7 Years
© A&C Black

Fundraisers

- **Work in a group.**
- **Discuss a way to raise money for a charity.**

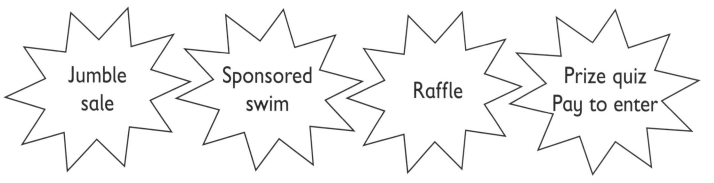

Jumble sale

Sponsored swim

Raffle

Prize quiz Pay to enter

- **Write notes about the good and bad points.**

We talked about _____

Good	Bad

NOW TRY THIS!

- **Why will your group's way of fundraising be good?**
- **Explain your answer to another group.**

Teachers' note First complete 'Charity choice: 1 and 2' in order to choose a charity to support. The children can work in groups to discuss how to raise funds for it, choosing from the ones in the flashes or others suggested to them. What would make it a good method and what might be difficult? (See 'Fundraising plan'.)

A Lesson for Every Day
Literacy
6–7 Years
© A&C Black

Fundraising plan

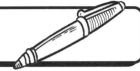

- **Work in a group.**
- **Plan a fundraising activity.**

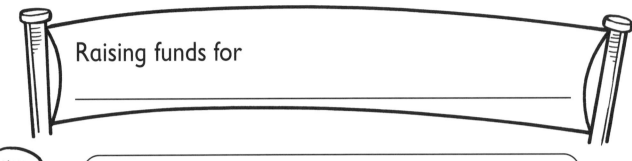

Raising funds for

_____

We are going to hold a _____

_____

This is how we shall do it.

Job	Who will do it

NOW TRY THIS!

- **Tell another group about your plan.**
- **Ask them for suggestions.**
- **Tell a teacher or other grown-up if you want to change your plan.**
- **Say how you would change it.**

Teachers' note First complete page 'Fundraisers'. The children should have discussed their choice of fundraising method with an adult, to ensure that it is feasible. This activity is suitable for groups of four, who should allocate all the tasks they have identified.

A Lesson for Every Day
Literacy
6-7 Years
© A&C Black

Moving day

- ## Talk about the picture.

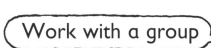
Work with a group

- ## Give the people names. Take a role each.

My name:

My role:

About my role:

- ## Act the story.

NOW TRY THIS!

What problem could one of the people have?
- ### Act the story.
- ### Show how the problem is solved.

Home sweet home

Teachers' note Each child will need a copy of this page. Encourage them to talk about their own experiences of moving house or of watching new neighbours arrive. Encourage them to think about what the girl in the picture might do after seeing the removal van arrive, and what she might say to the new arrivals. They should then enact a conversation in role.

A Lesson for Every Day
Literacy
6–7 Years
© A&C Black

- **Write the word they are thinking of.**

Use the word-bank.

This word has two syllables and four phonemes. It ends with a | y | that sounds like | ee |.

It has one syllable and three phonemes. It has | s | that sounds like | z |.

Word-bank

bread

gnat

rose

turned

very

It has one syllable and four phonemes. It has | ea | that sounds like | e |.

It has one syllable and three phonemes. It begins with | gn | that says | n |.

It has one syllable and four phonemes. It has an | ed | ending for the past tense.

NOW TRY THIS!

- **Describe these words.**

| h | ea | d | | b | ur | n | ed |

| p | ar | t | y | | d | u | mb |

Teachers' note Display a list of words: for example, *crying, cutter, post, treat*. Tell the children to work out which word you are thinking of from your clues: *It has two syllables.* (Clap twice and encourage them to do the same.) *It has four phonemes.* (Help them to count the phonemes in each word.) *It has a double letter before an -er ending*. Then invite a volunteer to describe a word from the list.

A Lesson for Every Day
Literacy
6-7 Years
© A&C Black

Mind-readers: 2

• **Write the word they are thinking of.**

Use the word-bank.

It has two syllables and four phonemes. It begins with $\boxed{w}$. It has an $\boxed{er}$ ending.

It has two syllables, five phonemes and a doubled letter before $\boxed{ing}$.

Word-bank

cracker

hopping

lamb

talked

water

It has one syllable, four phonemes, an $\boxed{or}$ sound spelled $\boxed{al}$ and an $\boxed{ed}$ ending for the past tense.

It has two syllables, five phonemes, two letters for one sound and an $\boxed{er}$ ending.

It has one syllable, three phonemes and ends with $\boxed{m}$ spelled $\boxed{mb}$.

NOW TRY THIS!

• **Describe these words.**

w	al	k	ed

kn	i	t

s	i	tt	i	ng

Teachers' note Display a list of words: for example, *crying, cutter, post, treat*. Tell the children to work out which word you are thinking of from your clues: *It has two syllables*. (Clap twice and encourage them to do the same.) *It has four phonemes*. (Help them to count the phonemes in each word.) *It has a double letter before an -er ending*. Then invite a volunteer to describe a word from the list.

A Lesson for Every Day
Literacy
6-7 Years
© A&C Black

83

What are you doing?

- **Read the question.**
- **Write the children's answers.**

What are you doing?

I am _____.

I am _____.

84

Teachers' note Ask the children to say what you are doing: standing, walking, pointing. Invite them to write the words on a wipe-off board (or display them on the interactive whiteboard). Remind them of the term *base word*. Cover the **-ing** ending and point out the base words *stand*, *walk* and *point* and ask the children how these words were changed.

A Lesson for Every Day
Literacy
6-7 Years
© A&C Black

Let's ask Rapunzel

- **Read the children's questions.**
- **Write Rapunzel's answers.**

What is in the tower?

1

What do you do apart from singing?

2

What did you do before the witch locked you in the tower?

3

1

_____

_____

_____

_____

_____

_____

_____

_____

2

_____

_____

_____

_____

_____

_____

_____

_____

3

_____

_____

_____

_____

NOW TRY THIS!

- **Write another question for Rapunzel.**
- **Give it to a friend to answer.**

Teachers' note This could be used to prepare for or to follow up a 'hot-seating' activity in which a volunteer acts as Rapunzel and the others ask her questions about her past, what happened to her and why, and about other characters in the story. The children could first talk in pairs about the story and what they would like to ask Rapunzel.

A Lesson for Every Day
Literacy
6-7 Years
© A&C Black

Faces

- **Look at the faces.**
- **Choose two words for each** **character** **.**

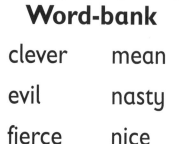

_____

_____

_____

_____

_____

_____

_____

NOW TRY THIS!

- **Look at a picture of another character.**
- **Write a sentence about the character's face.**

86

Teachers' note Ask the children if they can tell what a story character is like from pictures. They could discuss the faces on this page with a friend before they select words to describe him or her. Also discuss characters who look beautiful but are bad (for example, Snow White's wicked stepmother) and ugly characters who are good (for example, the Beast in *Beauty and the Beast*).

A Lesson for Every Day
Literacy
6-7 Years
© A&C Black

Our choice

- **Work with a group.**
- **Write notes about a book you all like.**

Books by the same author

Author _____

Title _____

Don't give away the ending!

Who the book is about

_____
_____
_____
_____

Other characters

_____
_____
_____
_____

The problem

_____
_____
_____
_____
_____

NOW TRY THIS!

- **Use your notes to help you to write a review about the book.**

Teachers' note In small groups, the children choose one book they all like by the same author. They name and describe the main character and other characters and say what happens in the story – without giving away the ending. They could summarise the problems faced by the characters and how they try to resolve them.

A Lesson for Every Day
Literacy
6-7 Years
© A&C Black

The story judge

Title _____

Author _____

Illustrator _____

Publisher _____

Key 😊 I like it very much.　😐 I think it is OK.　☹ I do not like it.

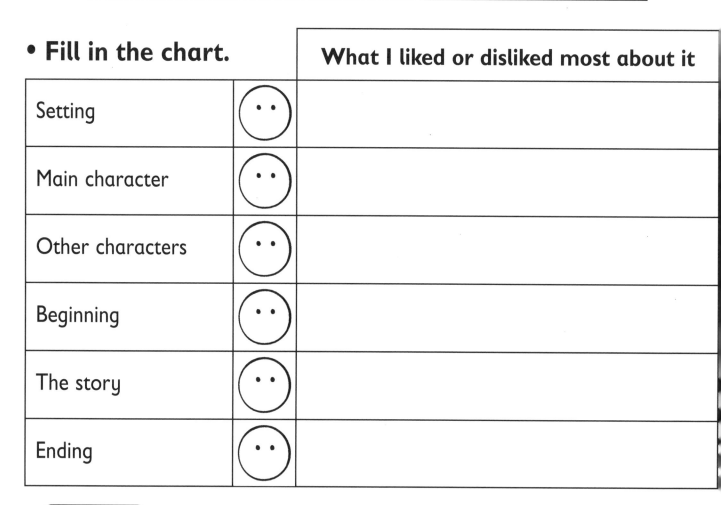

• **Fill in the chart.**

		What I liked or disliked most about it
Setting	😐	
Main character	😐	
Other characters	😐	
Beginning	😐	
The story	😐	
Ending	😐	

NOW TRY THIS!

• **Write a report to tell others why they should or shouldn't read this story.**

Teachers' note Use this to help the children to record their responses to a story by a significant children's author. Different children could focus on different stories and present their responses to the class.

A Lesson for Every Day
Literacy
6-7 Years
© **A&C Black**

Character swap: 1

This boy's cousin, Jenny, has come to stay. She is always playing jokes on him. What if a character from another story swapped places with him?

• **Make notes about this.**

Next morning as I lay in bed,
I was wary of the day
ahead with Jenny.

Would there be itching powder in my underwear?

Would the soap leave my face dirty?

Would my fried egg be made of plastic?

I felt rather nervous as I got dressed and washed.
But nothing dreadful happened. When I went downstairs
Jenny was already there.

I sat down very carefully. I wasn't going to be caught out again.

From *Jenny the Joker* by Colin West

New character _____

From (story) _____

What the character might do

_____

_____

_____

_____

Teachers' note The children need to read *Jenny the Joker* by Colin West (A&C Black). Who is the story about and what problem does the boy face? How does he try to resolve it? Ask the children to think of another story character who might try something different. Write notes about why they think this character might do this.

A Lesson for Every Day
Literacy
6-7 Years
© A&C Black

Character swap: 2

- **Rewrite the page from *Jenny the Joker*.**
- **Put your new character in it.**

Next morning as I lay in bed _____

_____

NOW TRY THIS!

- **Plan the rest of the story.**

What next?

Teachers' note The children first need to have completed 'Character swap: 1'. Invite volunteers to share their ideas about the new character they made up on 'Character swap: 1'. They can then write the next page of the story, beginning with the opening provided and adding illustrations (which could include speech bubbles). They could give the boy a name.

A Lesson for Every Day
Literacy
6-7 Years
© A&C Black

Today and yesterday

Today | I am going | to school.

Yesterday | I went | to school.

• Fill in the gaps.

Today I am playing football.

Yesterday _____ .

Today I am walking to school.

Yesterday _____ .

Today I am having a school dinner.

Yesterday _____ .

Today I am doing maths.

Yesterday _____ .

Today I am writing a story.

Yesterday _____ .

NOW TRY THIS!

- **Write sentences for today using these.**

  | eating | singing | watching |

- **Change the sentences to yesterday.**

Teachers' note Remind the children that we change the words for what we do depending on whether we are doing it now or have already done it. Read the completed example and demonstrate how to complete the first one. The children could give other examples of their own. You could link this with word-level work on the ways in which words change according to meaning.

A Lesson for Every Day
Literacy
6–7 Years
© A&C Black

- **Watch a DVD or television programme about a seaside place.**
- **Write some important facts about the place in the shells.**

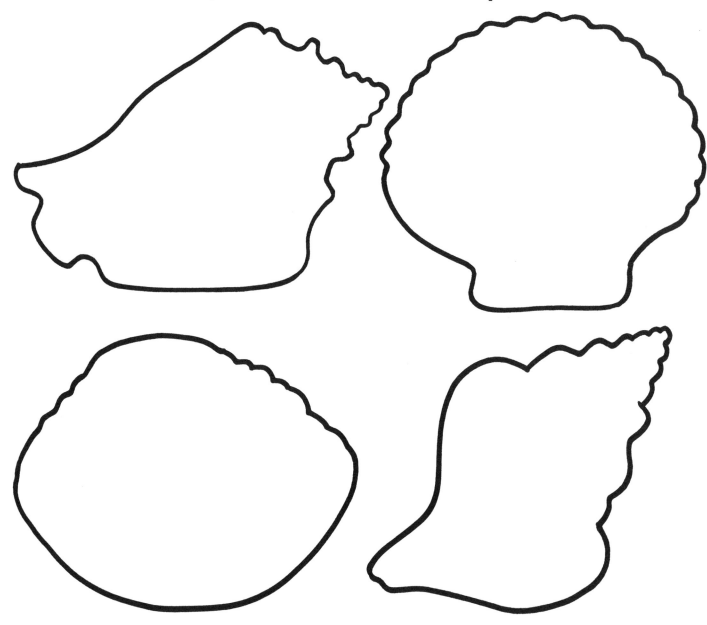

NOW TRY THIS!

- **How did the DVD or programme show what was important?**
- **Tell a partner.**

Think about zooming, voice, actions, music.

Teachers' note Tell the children that they are going to watch a television programme about a seaside place so that they can find out about the place. Remind them about 'good listening' and ask them to find out as much as they can about the place. If possible, let different groups watch programmes about different places and then present a talk about the place to the others.

A Lesson for Every Day
Literacy
6-7 Years
© A&C Black

Living picture

- **Work in a large group.**
- **Act a role in the picture.**

NOW TRY THIS!

- **What can you do to change what is happening in the picture?
Write on the chart.**

My character	
What I shall do	
What the others might do	

Teachers' note In groups of up to 11, the children should explore the roles of the people in the picture (supported by an adult if necessary). For the extension activity, encourage them to choose a character and to consider what he or she might do during the journey. Some children might find it easier to enact the scene and then record what happened, rather than using the chart for planning.

A Lesson for Every Day
Literacy
6–7 Years
© A&C Black

Base words with ing

• **Write the** base words .

Examples: creeping _creep_   sliding _slide_

pushing _____   charging _____

stopping _____   running _____

riding _____   studying _____

dancing _____   hopping _____

skipping _____   jumping _____

copying _____   diving _____

• **List the base words in three sets.**

Think about how they change to add ing .

①

②

③

NOW TRY THIS!

• **For each set of base words write a** rule **for adding** ing .

Teachers' note Remind them of the term base word. Ask them to watch and say what you are doing: sitting, clapping, writing. Write each of these along with its base word and ask the children how the base word has been changed. Compare these with the changes when the suffix -ed is added to form the past tense.

A Lesson for Every Day
Literacy
6-7 Years
© A&C Black

In the air

- **Which is the correct** | spelling |**?**
- **Write the word in the gap.**

bear   bare

At the zoo we saw a _____.

Jake had _____ feet.

fair   fare

We had fun at the _____.

I paid my bus _____.

? where   wear

_____ are you going?

I'll _____ my trainers.

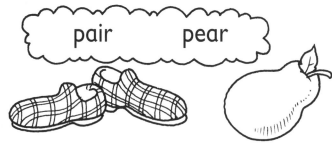

pair   pear

There is a _____ of slippers.

That is a nice juicy _____.

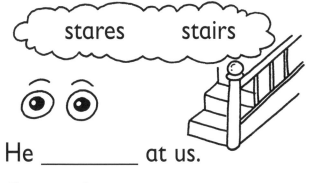

stares   stairs

He _____ at us.

Go up the _____.

herd   heard

There's a _____ of cows.

He _____ a scream.

NOW TRY THIS!

- **Write two sentences using these.**

| hair | | hare |

Teachers' note Model how to complete the first example by reading the sentences and supplying the missing words (orally). Repeat this and ask the children to point to the picture that shows the correct meaning of *bare/bear*, then ask them if they know which spelling is correct. They could use mnemonics to help: for example, A *bear* has *ears* or My feet *are* bare.

A Lesson for Every Day
Literacy
6–7 Years
© A&C Black

Character quest

- **Write what you know about a** | character |.

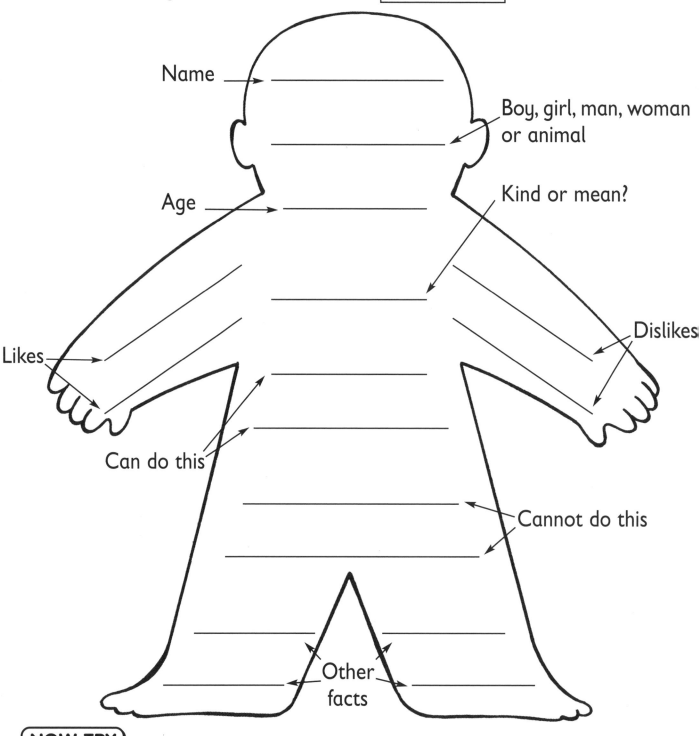

Name — _____

Boy, girl, man, woman or animal ← _____

Age — _____

Kind or mean? ↙ _____

Likes → _____

Dislikes ← _____

Can do this ↗ _____

Cannot do this ← _____

Other facts _____

- **What else would you like to know about the character?**
- **Write a question.**

96

Teachers' note This page could support work on a character who appears in either one or several books by an author. Enlarge the page to A3 or display it on an interactive whiteboard to use it with a group. The character outline helps the children to record different aspects of the character in an organised way.

A Lesson for Every Day
Literacy
6-7 Years
© A&C Black

Reasons

Title <u>A Necklace of Raindrops</u>

Author <u>Joan Aiken</u>

- **Why did it happen?**
- **Write the** | reason |.

The North Wind gave Laura a necklace of raindrops	because >	
Laura had to take off the necklace	because >	
A fish, a bird and a mouse promised to find the necklace	because >	
The King of Arabia said Laura could have her necklace back	so that >	

NOW TRY THIS!

- **Describe another important event in the story.**
- **Write why it happened.**

Teachers' note This page supports discussion of the main events of a story, focusing on why they happened. You could use the software on the enclosed CD-ROM to adapt the sheet by blanking out part so that it can be used with another story (or copy it onto a whiteboard and use the eraser).

A Lesson for Every Day
Literacy
6-7 Years
© A&C Black

Character clues

- **What are the** [characters] **like?**
- **Fill in the gaps.**

Mrs Smark stared at him from behind the counter. Her top lip curled up at the side as she slid the parcel across the table.

Mrs Smark is _____

Old Jim had a round face that reminded Ella of a big red apple. His twinkling brown eyes danced as he smiled at her.

Old Jim is _____

Mr Scratchit was scraping around in his garden as usual, muttering to himself. His bony elbows poked out of holes in his jumper. I was glad I could only see the back of him because his sharp, narrow, blue eyes scared me.

Mr Scratchit is _____

Nina rested her hand on Natalie's arm and looked at her gently. "Don't cry," she said "You can come and stay with us while your mum is in hospital. We'll look after you."

Nina is _____

Leo ran along the path through the field. The match was due to start in five minutes But what was that noise? It was coming from the pond. Maybe someone had fallen in. Leo stepped though the long grass and pushed the bushes apart. There was the pond. A hand and a head came up through the water. Leo had to act fast.

Leo is _____

NOW TRY THIS!

- **Circle the words in the stories which tell you what the characters are like.**

Teachers' note Read the first passage with the children and invite comments about what Mrs Smark is like. Encourage the children to say why they think this and to quote words from the text which give them this impression. They could compare the passage with a description such as 'Mrs Smark, the shopkeeper, was nasty.' Which helps them best to imagine Mrs Smark?

A Lesson for Every Day
Literacy
6-7 Years
© A&C Black

Story settings

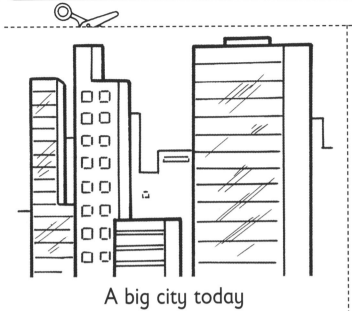

A big city today

A big city in the future

A tiny village in the mountains

A village long ago

Under the ground

In a space city

Teachers' note The children should first have read or listened to a story by a significant children's author and talked about the setting. Tell them that they are going to prepare to write their own longer story and that first they are going to choose a setting. See also 'Story character'.

A Lesson for Every Day
Literacy
6–7 Years
© A&C Black

99

Story character

- **Make up a story character.**
- **Draw the character.**
- **Write in the speech bubbles.**

My name is
_____ .

I am _____
years old.

I live in
_____
with _____
_____
_____ .

I enjoy _____
_____
best of all.

I am good at
_____
_____
_____ .

My friends
are _____
_____
_____
_____
_____ .

I am not so
good at _____
_____
_____
_____ .

NOW TRY THIS!

- **Write the beginning of a story.**
- **Introduce your characters.**

Teachers' note Use this with 'Story settings'. Ask the children to think about characters for their story setting. They could complete this as a 'hot-seating' activity with a partner asking them about their character.

A Lesson for Every Day
Literacy
6-7 Years
© A&C Black

The wish

- Imagine your story character has a wish.
- Write notes about it.

Who granted the wish?

Why?

Where?

What was the wish?

NOW TRY THIS!

- **Act the scene with a friend.**

Teachers' note As well as planning their own story, they could use this page to analyse a story they have recently read. See also 'The wish dialogue'.

A Lesson for Every Day
Literacy
6–7 Years
© A&C Black

The wish dialogue

- **Imagine the scene of the wish.**
- **Write the story.**

Use your notes.

Write sentences.

What your character was doing

Where

What it was like

_____
_____
_____
_____
_____
_____

Who came

What this character was like

What he or she said and did

_____
_____
_____
_____
_____

The wish

_____
_____
_____
_____

Teachers' note The children should first complete 'The wish' in which they plan an extended story about a wish. Ask them to describe the scene in which the character is granted a wish and to write what the characters did and said. See also 'The wish consequences'.

A Lesson for Every Day
Literacy
6-7 Years
© A&C Black

The wish consequences

What happened because of the wish?
- **Write notes.**

I wish _____

_____

_____

_____
_____
_____
_____

Problems

_____
_____
_____

Solution

_____
_____

Teachers' note The children should first complete 'The wish' and 'The wish dialogue'. Ask them about the notes they made (page 109) for a story about a wish. What happened because of the wish? They should first write the wish and then how it came true and what unexpected things happened.

A Lesson for Every Day
Literacy
6-7 Years
© A&C Black

Past mistakes

This is right ☑.

Today I wait

Yesterday I waited

This is wrong ☒.

Today I eat

Yesterday I eated

Are these right or wrong? ☑ or ☒

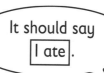 It should say I ate.

Today I skip.
Yesterday I skipped.

Today I speak.
Yesterday I speaked.

Today I write.
Yesterday I writed.

Today I sing.
Yesterday I singed.

Today I dance.
Yesterday I danced.

Today I go.
Yesterday I goed.

 **NOW TRY THIS!**

- **Copy the wrong words.**
- **Write them correctly.**

_____ ✗ _____ ✗ _____ ✗ _____ ✗

_____ ✔ _____ ✔ _____ ✔ _____ ✔

Teachers' note Remind the children of their previous learning about the changes we make to 'doing' words depending on whether we are doing it now or have already done it. Introduce the terms past and present. Read the completed example to the children before giving them a copy of the page. Ask them which examples are correct and what is wrong with *I eated*.

A Lesson for Every Day
Literacy
6–7 Years
© A&C Black

- **The words in boxes are wrong.**
- **Write the correct words.**

Our day at the zoo

First we went to see the monkeys.

They | are playing | _____ on ropes.

We | watch | _____ them for a while. Then we went to

the elephant house. An elephant | squirts | _____ water

everywhere. It | is | _____ fun. Our teacher got soaked.

A tiger | growls | _____ and scared us, but the lions

| take | _____ no notice of us. It started to

rain just as we got into the bus to come back.

NOW TRY THIS!

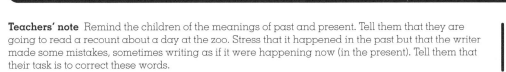

- **Write three sentences about your favourite day out.**

Teachers' note Remind the children of the meanings of past and present. Tell them that they are going to read a recount about a day at the zoo. Stress that it happened in the past but that the writer made some mistakes, sometimes writing as if it were happening now (in the present). Tell them that their task is to correct these words.

A Lesson for Every Day
Literacy
6–7 Years
© A&C Black

Caterpillar talk

- **Work with a group.**
- **Say 'caterpillar' in different ways.**

Make it sound sleepy.

Make it sound bad-tempered.

Make it sound cheerful.

Make it sound lively.

NOW TRY THIS!

- **Read a page of dialogue with a partner.**
- **Change your voice to match what the character says.**

Each read the words spoken by a different character.

Teachers' note Model the first example, emphasising the sleepy mood, and encourage the children to do the same. Invite volunteers who do this effectively to demonstrate it for the others. Let them try again. Ask them to practise the other examples with their groups and then invite groups to demonstrate. Which feeling are they expressing in 'caterpillar talk'?

A Lesson for Every Day
Literacy
6–7 Years
© A&C Black

How well did you speak?

My name _____

- **Draw a face in each box.** ☺, ☺ **or** ☹
- **Write one thing you could do better each time.**

For your teacher

Date _____

Activity _____

	I spoke clearly.	☐
	I could do better if I _____ _____	
	I looked at people.	☐
	I could do better if I _____ _____	
	I made my voice sound interesting.	☐
	I could do better if I _____ _____	
	I used my face, arms and hands.	☐
	I could do better if I _____ _____	

This is what I did best.

Teachers' note This page could be used to support a 'jigsawing' activity in which some children listen to a partner speaking (and, of course, some must speak). The listeners then speak to another group about what their partner said. During other sessions they could swap roles.

A Lesson for Every Day
Literacy
6-7 Years
© A&C Black

107

A famous person

- **Plan a talk about a famous person.**

Person's name	What he or she is famous for
_____	_____
Year of birth _____	_____
Is he or she still alive?	_____
_____	_____
	_____
	_____
Birthplace _____	Important events in the person's life
_____	_____
Schooldays _____	_____
_____	_____
_____	_____
_____	_____

NOW TRY THIS!

- **Tell your group about the person.**
- **Make your talk sound interesting.**

Use your voice to sound

… excited…

… as if you are wondering…

… surprised…

Teachers' note Ask the children to find out about people connected with other work: for example, in RE, citizenship or history. Different groups could present talks about different people. Remind the children about 'good listening': looking at the speaker, thinking as well as listening and asking questions afterwards. Ask each audience what they learned about the person.

A Lesson for Every Day
Literacy
6–7 Years
© A&C Black

A day out

- **Ask a partner about a day out.**
- **Write the answers in the speech bubbles.**

Where did you go for your day out?

What did you do there?

What did you like best about it?

If you went there again, what would you change?

NOW TRY THIS!

- **Ask your partner two other questions about the day out.**
- **Write the answers.**

Teachers' note The children should work in pairs, with one telling the other about a day out and the listener asking questions and making brief notes of the answers to remind themselves of what was said. During another lesson they could swap roles. This could be part of a 'jigsawing' activity in which the children tell another group about their friend's day out.

A Lesson for Every Day
Literacy
6–7 Years
© A&C Black

A class pet

- **What would be a good pet for your class?**
- **Talk with your group.**
- **Write the group's ideas in the boxes.**

- **Each find out about a pet.**
- **Write notes on the notepad.**

Pet _____

What it needs

Home	Bed	Food	Care

NOW TRY THIS!

- **Tell your group why this pet would be good.**
- **Listen to their ideas.**

Teachers' note It should be made clear to the children whether they can really choose a class pet or whether they are just considering which animals are suitable for keeping at school. They could find out about the needs of a pet from information books, leaflets from vets or pet shops or from organisations such as the RSPCA, PDSA, Dogs Trust or Cat Protection League.

A Lesson for Every Day
Literacy
6-7 Years
© A&C Black

Picture clues

- **Read the words.**
- **Look at the tricky parts.**
- **Cover the words. Then write them.**

The pictures will help.

---

shoe	busy	balloon
The <u>shoe</u> <u>shon</u>e.	It's a <u>busy</u> <u>bus</u>.	There's a <u>ball</u> in the <u>ball</u>oon.
		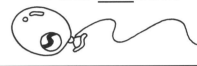

often	family	across
I <u>often</u> think <u>of</u> <u>ten</u>.	<u>I</u>'m in my fam<u>il</u>y.	There's <u>a</u> <u>cross</u> <u>across</u> the page.

friend	sign	eye
<u>I</u>'m your fr<u>iend</u> to the <u>end</u>.	There's a <u>g</u> in the si<u>g</u>n.	Look at my <u>ee</u> <u>eye</u>s.

NOW TRY THIS!

- **Draw pictures and write sentences to help you to spell these.**

| office | knee | grey |

Teachers' note Read the first example with the children and show them how the word shone helps them to remember the unusual spelling of shoe. Point out that the picture helps them to remember this. Ask them how the bus helps them to spell busy. The children could keep a list of words they find tricky. Provide a small notebook with pages headed with the letters of the alphabet for this.

A Lesson for Every Day
Literacy
6-7 Years
© A&C Black

Base words with ful

- **Write the** base words **in the gaps.**

Examples:

This cut is **painful**.
It causes <u>pain</u>.

I am being **careful**.
I am taking <u>care</u>.

I am **cheerful**.
I am full of

_____.

It is good to be
helpful. You can

_____.

My toolbox is **useful**.
It always has a

_____.

Jed is a **playful**
dog. He likes to

_____.

I try to be **truthful**.
I try to tell the

_____.

I am **hopeful** about
the weather.
I am full of _____.

A **skilful** artist painted
it. She used a lot of

_____.

I am **dutiful**.
I do my

_____.

NOW TRY THIS!

- **Sort the** ful **words into sets.**

Think about
how the base
word changes.

Teachers' note Introduce another suffix for adjectives: **-ful**. Display some examples and ask them to identify the base words: *thankful, painful, faithful*. Point out that very few base words change before adding **-ful** and show some exceptions: *pitiful, dutiful, beautiful, skilful*.

A Lesson for Every Day
Literacy
6–7 Years
© A&C Black

Hide and seek

- **Draw the gnome family in the picture.**
- **Colour them in.**

Norman Gnome
Follow the path until you come to a bridge.
Look under the bridge.

Norma Gnome
Follow the path.
Cross the bridge.
Keep on the path.
Look in the house.

Nora Gnome
Go to the tallest tree.
Cross the path.
Look behind the bushes.

Noah Gnome
Follow the path until you come to a fence.
Go through the gate.
Follow the path until you come to a pond.
Look in the boat.

START

A Lesson for Every Day
Literacy
6-7 Years
© A&C Black

NOW TRY THIS!

- **Hide something small.**
- **Write** | instructions | **for a friend to find it.**

 a shell   a ball   a marble   a coin

Teachers' note Read the first piece of text with the children and help them to follow the instructions. Ask if they are good instructions. Point out that instructions tell the reader what they need and what they should do (in the correct order). The children can then read and follow the rest of the instructions.

113

Ladybird program

- **Read the** [instructions].
- **Draw the ladybird in the correct square.**

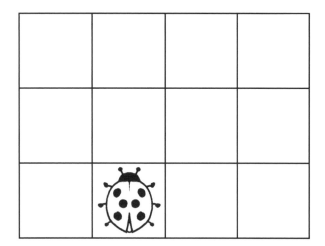

Go forward one square.

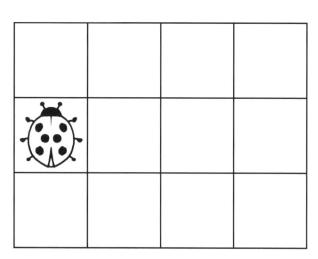

Go back one square.

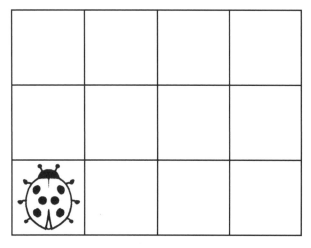

Go forward two squares.

Turn right.

Go forward one square.

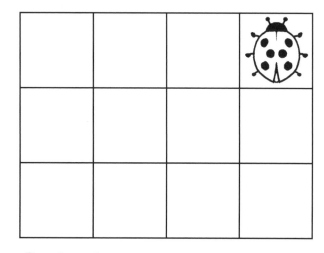

Go back one square.

Turn left.

Go forward three squares.

NOW TRY THIS!

- **Does the** [order] **of the instructions matter?**
- **Find out with a friend.**

Teachers' note Ensure that the children know which directions are meant by *forward, back, left* and *right*. You could write these on the page and add arrows to show the directions. Invite a volunteer to read the first instruction and to point out the square the ladybird will end on. The children can then draw the ladybird in this square and do the same for the subsequent instructions.

A Lesson for Every Day
Literacy
6–7 Years
© A&C Black

Stripy lolly

- **Fill in the gaps.**

You need

pomegranate juice

lolly stick

lemonade

clear yogurt pot

orange juice

freezer

orange

white

red

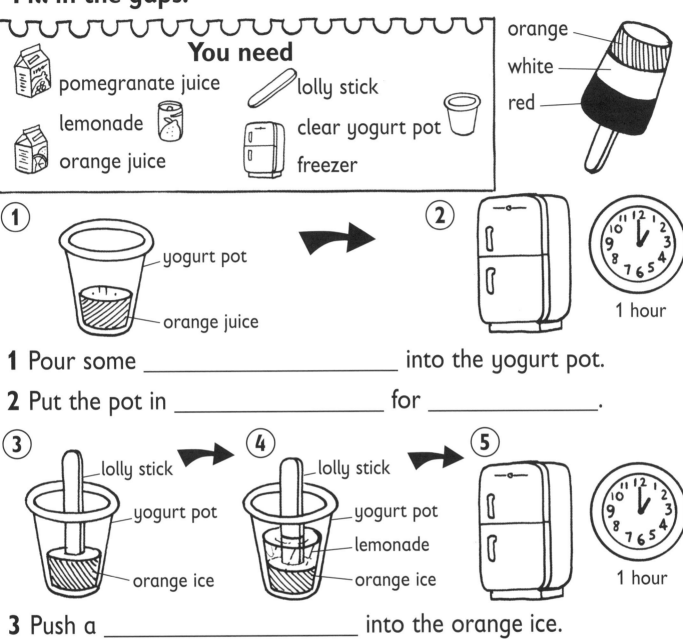

1 yogurt pot

orange juice

2 1 hour

1 Pour some _____ into the yogurt pot.

2 Put the pot in _____ for _____.

3 lolly stick

yogurt pot

orange ice

4 lolly stick

yogurt pot

lemonade

orange ice

5 1 hour

3 Push a _____ into the orange ice.

4 Pour _____ into the yogurt pot.

5 _____.

NOW TRY THIS!

- **Predict** | instructions | **6 and 7.**
- **Draw and label the pictures.**
- **Write the instructions.**

Teachers' note Ask the children to read the instructions with a friend. Ask them what the instructions are for and what they need to make the lolly. Point out the 'instruction words' (verbs in the imperative) and remind the children that words like this tell the reader what to do. Compare them with the sentence structure of a recount: 'I poured some orange juice into the yogurt pot.'

A Lesson for Every Day
Literacy
6–7 Years
© A&C Black

Do as I say

- **Choose a row of pictures.**
- **Look at the pictures. Choose one.**
- **Tell your friend what to do.**
- **Then say, 'Go!'**

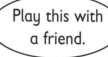 Play this with a friend.

NOW TRY THIS!

- **Make up a list of five instructions for a friend to follow.**

Teachers' note Begin by giving some simple instructions for different children to follow: for example, Stand up, Clap your hands, Nod your head. Continue using signs only: for example, Stand up, Turn around and so on. Ask the children to cut out the pictures and choose one. They tell a friend what to do without showing the picture.

A Lesson for Every Day
Literacy
6–7 Years
© A&C Black

Make this

- **Choose a pattern.**
- **List the shapes in it.**
- **Tell a friend how to make it.**

Don't let your friend see which one it is.

You need	You need	You need
_____	_____	_____
_____	_____	_____
_____	_____	_____
_____	_____	_____

You need	You need	You need
_____	_____	_____
_____	_____	_____
_____	_____	_____
_____	_____	_____

Teachers' note The children need plastic, card or paper shapes similar to those in the pictures. They cut out the pictures and choose one. They list the shapes needed, then read this out to a friend, telling them how to make the picture without showing it. To evaluate their instructions they could compare their friend's picture with the original. They could also add colours (see the notes on the activity on page 18).

A Lesson for Every Day
Literacy
6–7 Years
© A&C Black

117

Treasure hunt

Play this with a friend.
You each need a page like this.
- **Choose where to**
  hide the treasure.

Don't let your friend see your page.

- **Give instructions for finding the treasure.**

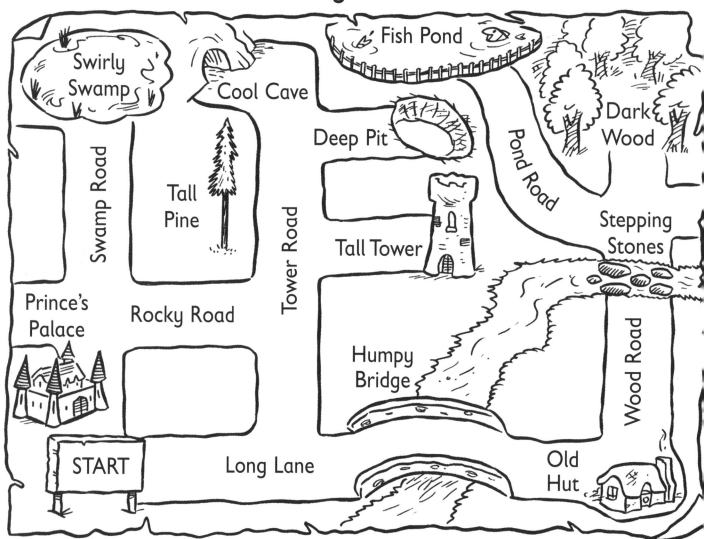

Swirly Swamp

Cool Cave

Fish Pond

Dark Wood

Deep Pit

Pond Road

Swamp Road

Tall Pine

Tower Road

Tall Tower

Stepping Stones

Prince's Palace

Rocky Road

Humpy Bridge

Wood Road

START

Long Lane

Old Hut

 118

Teachers' note Read the names of the places with the children. Ask them to choose one of these as a hiding place for the treasure. They give instructions from 'Start' to tell their friend the way to the treasure. The friend could use a counter or draw a line to keep track of the route. Model how to do this, perhaps using a copy on an interactive whiteboard.

A Lesson for Every Day
Literacy
6-7 Years
© A&C Black

Sand pie

Kerry wants to know how to make a sand pie.

- **Answer her questions.**

What do I need?

You need _____ ☺
_____
_____

Should the sand be dry, damp or very wet?

It _____ ☺
_____

What shall I do first?

First _____ ☺
_____

Then what shall I do?

_____ ☺
_____
_____

What shall I do next?

_____ ☺
_____
_____

How can I make it come out of the bucket?

Then _____ ☺
_____

NOW TRY THIS!

- **Read your answers with a friend.**
- **Write better instructions.**

Teachers' note The children will probably be familiar with making sand pies but let them practise using a sand tray. Ask them to say what they are using and what they are doing. They could take turns to tell a partner what they are doing, then repeat the activity – one child telling the other what to do.

A Lesson for Every Day
Literacy
6-7 Years
© A&C Black

How to light a bulb

- **Write instructions for lighting a bulb.**

You need

1

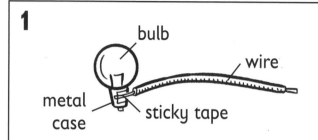

bulb
wire
metal case
sticky tape

_____

_____

_____

_____

2

bulb
wire
sticky tape
metal case
sticky tape
battery

_____

_____

_____

_____

3

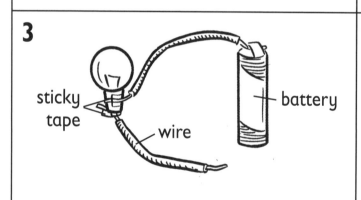

sticky tape
battery
wire

_____

_____

_____

_____

4

battery
wire
sticky tape

_____

_____

_____

_____

NOW TRY THIS!

- **What else might someone need to know about picture 4?**

Write on another piece of paper.

Teachers' note This should be used after the science activity where the children try to light a bulb using only a bulb, a battery, two wires and some sticky tape. Ask them to say what they used and what they did, then take turns to tell a partner what to do before writing these instructions. Their partners should do only what they are told.

A Lesson for Every Day
Literacy
6–7 Years
© A&C Black

This is a question mark.
It goes at the end of a question.

?

• **Read the sentences. Are they questions?** ✔ **or** ✗

This is a lion.

Where is my teddy?

Where are you going?

What time is it?

I like ice cream.

It is six o'clock.

• **Circle the question marks.**

NOW TRY THIS!

• **Write three questions.**
• **Put question marks at the end of them.**

Teachers' note Remind the children of their work on full stops. Tell them that some sentences ask a question and that these end with a question mark. They could practise drawing full stops at the right size and on the line on which they write. They can then read the sentences and decide whether they ask a question.

A Lesson for Every Day
Literacy
6-7 Years
© A&C Black

Question queen

- **Show the question queen where to put question marks.**
- **Show her where to put full stops.**

When can we go to the beach

Why is the sky blue

We can go there today

I like to play tennis

What shall we do

Where is the ball

Shall we play ball

Who is that boy

It is in the box

It's too cold to go to the beach

NOW TRY THIS!

- **Write two questions.**
- **Write the answers.**
  Remember | . | and | ? | .

Teachers' note The children should first have completed 'Question mark'. Ask them if the first
sentence is a question. What does it ask? Ask them where the sentence ends and if they should put
a full stop or a question mark at the end of it. They can then read the other sentences and decide
whether they should end with a question mark or a full stop.

A Lesson for Every Day
Literacy
6-7 Years
© A&C Black

Email check

• **Put in the full stops and questions marks.**

Lara :-)

Thanks for your email. I'm much better now I'm going back to school tomorrow Are your brothers back yet

How did you get on in the swimming gala I hope you had a good time I'm going to a swimming club next week I've got a new swimsuit

It's half term next week We're going to Wales Nan and Grandad are coming too We've booked a cottage by the sea Have you been to Wales

Can you come to our house when we get back Ask your mum

Love Annie x

NOW TRY THIS!

• **Write a short reply from Lara to Annie.**
• **Put some questions in it.**

Teachers' note Review the children's understanding of full stops and question marks. Tell them that they are going to read an email which someone sent without reading it through to check it. Explain that the full stops and question marks are missing and that their task is to put them in. Remind them that a sentence is not the same as a line of writing.

A Lesson for Every Day
Literacy
6-7 Years
© A&C Black

Hat test

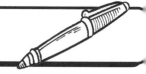

- **Look at the pictures and read how the children planned a fair test.**
- **Talk about what they did and what they found out.**

 Which material will be the best for keeping your head dry?

 cotton

 polythene

 fleece

Fold the material like this.

Staple some tape onto each end.

It makes a hat, like this!

Then pour water over your head.

No – put it on a teddy bear. I don't want to get wet.

Yes, then we can feel the teddy's head to see if it's wet.

We need to make all the hats the same size.

Yes, and use a watering can so it's like rain.

- **Why did they decide to use a teddy?**
- **Why did they need to make the hats the same size?**
- **What material will be the best for keeping the teddy dry?**
- **How did they work together?**

NOW TRY THIS!

- **How did working as a group help?**
- **Talk to your group.**
- **List the ways it helped.**

Teachers' note The children are asked to talk about the hat test, but remind them that they should listen to one another and ensure that everyone in the group joins in. Point out that they can help one another by asking 'What do you think?'

A Lesson for Every Day
Literacy
6–7 Years
© A&C Black

Rain hat test talk

• **Plan a talk about the rain hat test.**

The children were trying to find out _____

_____ .

They tested three materials:

1 _____ 2 _____ 3 _____

This is what they did:

First they folded _____

and stapled _____ .

Next they put a _____ on a _____ .

Then they _____

_____

_____ .

They made sure _____ .

To find out how well each hat worked they _____

_____ .

If the teddy bear's head was _____
it was a good rain hat.

NOW TRY THIS!

• **Record your talk.**
• **Play it back.**
• **Listen with a partner.**
• **Record it again if you can do better.**

Teachers' note The children should first have completed 'Hat test'. At another time, they could present their talk to a group that has not completed this or 'Hat test'. Focus on the listeners. After the talk they could question the speaker.

A Lesson for Every Day
Literacy
6-7 Years
© A&C Black

Make and write

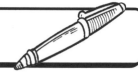

- **Watch a television programme about how to make something.**
- **Fill in the questionnaire.**

Title of programme

_____

What did the programme show you?

_____

How easy was this to make?

Difficult ☐

Not too difficult ☐

Easy ☐

Very easy ☐

What materials were used?

Paper or card ☐

Cloth or thread ☐

Empty containers or packets ☐

Beads or sequins ☐

Other ☐

How easy was it to get the materials?

Difficult ☐

Not too difficult ☐

Easy ☐

Very easy ☐

How easy was it to make the object?

Difficult ☐

Not too difficult ☐

Easy ☐

Very easy ☐

NOW TRY THIS!

- **How could the programme be improved?**
- **Make it surprising.**

Talk to a partner about it.

126

Teachers' note Let the children watch a television programme, DVD or video that shows how to make something. Provide materials so that they can make the artefact. Encourage them to talk about how useful the programme was. Ask if they have any difficulties in making the object and how the programme could have helped them.

A Lesson for Every Day
Literacy
6–7 Years
© A&C Black

At home in the past

- **Listen to a grown-up talking about homes when they were young.**
- **What was the same as now? What was different?**
- **Write about it on the house.**

Write notes.

Heating _____

_____

_____

Bedrooms _____

_____

_____

_____

Cleaning

_____

_____

_____

_____

_____

_____

Bathroom _____

_____

_____

_____

Living room _____

_____

_____

_____

_____

_____

Kitchen _____

_____

_____

_____

_____

_____

NOW TRY THIS!

- **What else would you like to know about homes in the past?**
- **Ask a question.**
- **Write the question and the answer.**

Teachers' note Invite an older person to come to talk to the children about home-life in his or her childhood. The speaker could highlight and describe differences such as the absence of computers and similarities the children might not be aware of, such as vacuum cleaners and television.

A Lesson for Every Day
Literacy
6–7 Years
© A&C Black

On the road

- **Listen to a talk about road safety.**
- **Tick the questions it answers.**
- **After the talk, choose a question to ask.**

If someone else asks a question, listen to the answer.

Where there is no crossing what should you do first before crossing a road? ☐

What should you do before you step off the pavement? ☐

What should you do while you are crossing the road? ☐

Where should you not cross a road? ☐

How can you stay safe near roads in the dark? ☐

What should you do at a pelican crossing? ☐

NOW TRY THIS!

- **Write the answers to the questions.**

Teachers' note Invite a road safety officer to give the children a short talk, or show them a video on road safety. They should listen carefully so that they can answer questions about the topic.

A Lesson for Every Day
Literacy
6-7 Years
© A&C Black

Welcome

- **I**magine someone new is going to join your class.
- **H**ow will you welcome them?
- **T**alk to your group.
- **W**rite your ideas on the welcome mats.

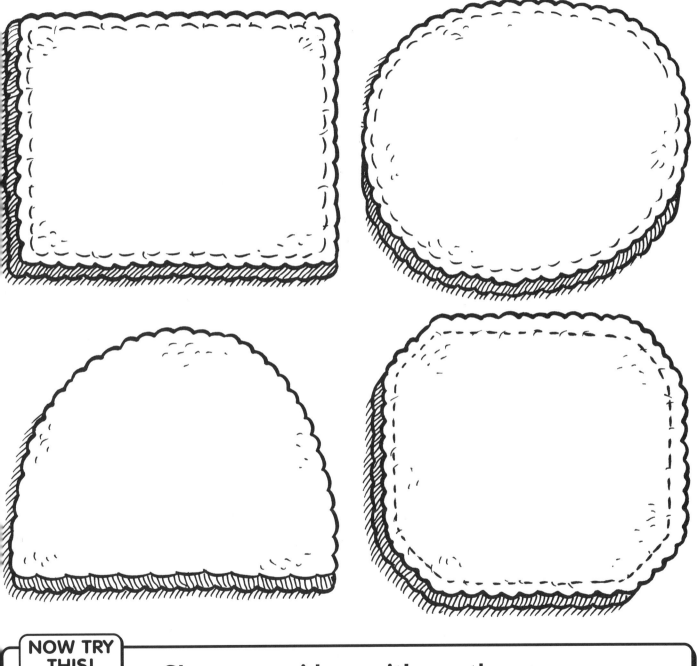

NOW TRY THIS!

- **S**hare your ideas with another group.

Teachers' note This page could be used to prepare for a new child joining the class. Help them to encourage each member of the group to contribute by asking questions such as *What do you think? What would make you feel welcome? How would that help?*

A Lesson for Every Day
Literacy
6–7 Years
© A&C Black

Remember, remember

• **Write a sentence for each letter. Draw a picture.**

Examples: **beauty**   **B**ig   **laugh**   **L**ook

Big
ears
are
useful
to
you.

Look
at
ugly
gorillas
howling.

cough	**C**_____	people	**P**_____
	o _____		**e** _____
	u _____		**o** _____
	g _____		**p** _____
	h _____.		**l** _____
			e _____.
equal	**E**_____	castle	**C**_____
	q _____		**a** _____
	u _____		**s** _____
	a _____		**t** _____
	l _____.		**l** _____
			e _____.

NOW TRY THIS!

• **Cover the words on this page.**
• **Write the words.**

Teachers' note Point out the completed examples and ask the children to read each sentence aloud, pointing to the initial letter of each word. Explain that it helps if the sentence has something to do with the meaning of the word. It could even begin with the word it helps with: for example, *Coughing outdoors upsets green hedges* or *Cough only under great handkerchiefs.*

130

A Lesson for Every Day
Literacy
6-7 Years
© A&C Black

Plurals wordsearch

- **(Loop) the words that mean more than one of these.**
- **Tick each word as you find its plural.** ✔

The first has been done for you.

bike ✔	jeep	taxi
bus	lorry	truck
car	tanker	van

t	r	u	c	k	s	l	z
a	a	v	a	n	s	o	b
n	d	x	r	f	c	r	b
k	b	u	s	e	s	r	l
e	i	m	g	p	h	i	k
r	k	n	s	t	j	e	m
s	e	j	e	e	p	s	v
q	s	r	t	a	x	i	s

NOW TRY THIS!

- **How do most words change to make more than one?**
- **Tell a friend the** rule **.**

Teachers' note Begin with pairs of sentences containing singulars and plurals that can be demonstrated: for example, *Here is a book/Here are some books*, *There is a girl/There are some girls*. Continue but invite the children to complete the second sentence. Ask them which phoneme they added, then ask them to look for the plurals in the wordsearch.

A Lesson for Every Day
Literacy
6–7 Years
© A&C Black

Match and sort: plurals

cats	crates	glasses	beads
dishes	owls	benches	buses
sticks	boxes	brushes	baths
roses	churches	pictures	peaches
teachers	cliffs	towers	bungalows
matches	pianos	witches	crabs
plums	frogs	ledges	horses
bunches	hearths	porches	bosses

Teachers' note Ask the children about any changes they made to singular nouns before adding -**s**. Cut out the cards and ask the children to sort them into sets according to how the plural is made. Invite feedback and help them to formulate rules for plurals.

A Lesson for Every Day
Literacy
6–7 Years
© A&C Black

My favourite things

- **Fill in the gaps with the** | plurals | .

Use the spelling rules you know.

I have a <u>dog</u> named Moss.

I have four _____ named Sam, Zip, Red and Rory.

I shall eat a <u>slice</u> of cake.

I shall eat two _____ of cake.

I picked a <u>bunch</u> of flowers for Mum.

I picked two _____ of flowers, one for Mum and one for Nan.

What is my name? Have a <u>guess</u>.

What is my name? Have three _____.

I saw a <u>fox</u> in the woods.

I saw six _____ in the woods.

I shall grant you a <u>wish</u>.

I shall grant you three _____.

NOW TRY THIS!

- **Write two** | rules | **for making plurals.**

Teachers' note Ask the children about the rules they used for making plurals. You could help them to write and display these rules. They should use them to help with this page.

A Lesson for Every Day
Literacy
6–7 Years
© A&C Black

Sail away

• **Write** ai **or** ay **in the gaps.**

Example: S<u>ai</u>l aw<u>ay</u>, little boat.

"Let's pl____ ball," said K____.

I put a lump of cl____ on the tr____.

The r____n ran down the dr____n.

One d____ the Little Red Hen found
a gr____n of wheat.

Tod____ is the first of M____.

The teacher will s____,"Wake up
your br____ns."

NOW TRY THIS!

• **Write a** rule **for spelling** ai **or** ay **words.**

Teachers' note Remind the children of two ways of spelling the /ai/ phoneme – ai and ay – and display some words containing these phonemes: for example, *chain, main, paint, train, wait; hay, lay, pay, pray, stay*. Ask them to notice where in the word the /ai/ phoneme is and where it is spelled ay (at the end of a word). The grapheme ai is rarely seen at the end of an English word.

A Lesson for Every Day
Literacy
6-7 Years
© A&C Black

Dragon life cycle

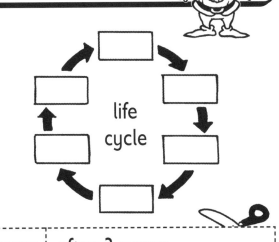

- **Cut out the pictures.**
- **Put them in order.**
- **Glue them onto paper.**
- **Draw arrows to link them.**
- **Tell the** | life cycle | **of a dragon.**

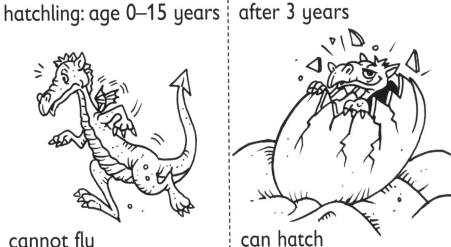

life cycle

wyrm: age 150–1500 years	hatchling: age 0–15 years	after 3 years

finds a mate/can lay eggs	cannot fly	can hatch
dragonet: age 16–90 years	a big green egg	adult: age 90–150 years

can fly	rocky ledge in a cave	can breathe fire

NOW TRY THIS!

- **Write one or two** | sentences | **to go with each picture.**

Teachers' note Explain that this is non-fiction – an information text, which gives information; it does not tell a story. Ask the children to pick out a picture of the beginning of a dragon's life and to describe it. They can then pick out the next picture and the next and so on, and put them in order. Point out the life cycle diagram and discuss why this is better than a flow-chart in a straight line.

A Lesson for Every Day
Literacy
6-7 Years
© A&C Black

Fairyland

• Fill in the gaps.

Why do fairies live at the bottom of the garden?

The fact-file will help.

Fairy fact-file

<u>Clothes</u>
made from flowers and leaves

○ <u>Shelter</u>
plants give shade and keep out rain
wings don't work when wet
wings melt in sunshine

○ <u>Food</u>
flowers and seeds

<u>Work</u>
tooth collection
fairytale writing

○

There are plants to give shelter from the _____ and the _____.

This keeps their _____ working and stops them melting.

Also there are plenty of _____ and _____ for them to eat.

Plants are also good for making _____.

NOW TRY THIS!

- **Why do fairies need to live near houses?**
- **Write an explanation.**

Think about their work.

Teachers' note Tell the children that this is a report, not a recount. Use examples to demonstrate the difference. They should use the fact-file to help them to fill the gaps and then use the completed report to help them to answer the question.

A Lesson for Every Day
Literacy
6–7 Years
© A&C Black

Buildings glossary: 1

	synagogue		cafe
	gurdwara		supermarket
	garage		barn
	library		house
	school		mandir
	leisure centre		factory
	mosque		church
	shop		office

Teachers' note The children could work in groups to help one another to read the words. This should be used with 'Buildings glossary: 2', each page being copied onto paper or card of a different colour. The cards should be cut out. The pages can be used in several ways (see 'Buildings glossary: 2').

A Lesson for Every Day
Literacy
6–7 Years
© A&C Black

137

Buildings glossary: 2

A farm building where hay is kept.	A place where people can sit and have a drink and something to eat.
A building where Christians worship.	A building where things are made.
A building where a car is kept.	A building where books are kept.
A building where Sikhs worship.	A building where people live.
A building where you can do sports such as swimming.	A building where Hindus worship.
A building where Muslims worship.	A building where people work at desks.
A building where children go to learn.	A building where you can buy things.
A very big building where you can buy food and other things.	A building where Jews worship.

Teachers' note Use this with 'Buildings glossary: 1'. Introduce the term definition as in dictionary or glossary definitions. The children could work as a group, matching the definitions to the words or they could place the cards face down and turn over a card from each set to play 'matching pairs', with the winner being the one with the most cards when all have been turned over.

A Lesson for Every Day
Literacy
6–7 Years
© A&C Black

What makes them go?

What make the toys go?

mouse

dog

buggy

police car

cart

truck

train

pram

- **Write the missing headings.**
- **List the toys on the chart.**

What makes them go?

Push	Clockwork		

NOW TRY THIS!

- **Make a chart to show what makes these go.**

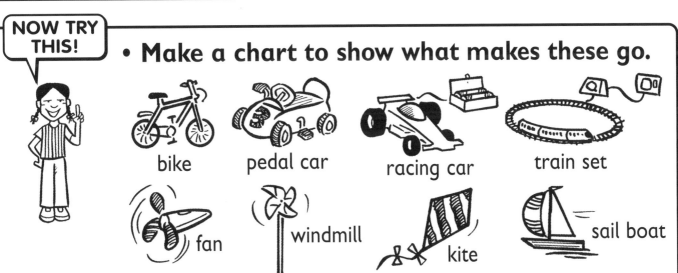

bike

pedal car

racing car

train set

fan

windmill

kite

sail boat

Teachers' note Ask the children to look at the pictures and say what they know about what makes each toy move. Does someone push them? Is there a clockwork motor to push them? What else can make things move? (For example, a battery-powered motor to push them or someone pulling).

A Lesson for Every Day
Literacy
6-7 Years
© A&C Black

Garden animals glossary

- **List the animals in the glossary below.**
- **Describe them.**

A glossary is in alphabetical order.

spider

woodlouse

snail

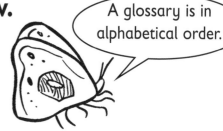

butterfly

Animal

What does it look like? How many legs? Wings?

NOW TRY THIS!

- **Use a computer to make a bigger glossary of garden animals.**

140

Teachers' note The children should first have used glossaries in information books and should know that the words are arranged in alphabetical order and that the glossary explains what they mean. They should have observed small garden animals.

A Lesson for Every Day
Literacy
6-7 Years
© A&C Black

Making music

How do you make sounds with these?

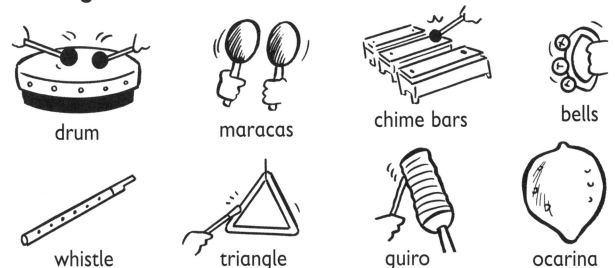

drum maracas chime bars bells

whistle triangle guiro ocarina

- **Write headings on the chart.**
- **List the instruments on it.**

How do you make sounds with these?

Blow			

Teachers' note The children first need to use the instruments shown in the pictures and to say what they do in order to make a sound with the instrument. Let them demonstrate and, if necessary, introduce words such as *tap*, *shake*, *blow* and *scrape*. They can then use the chart to help them to explain how each instrument works.

A Lesson for Every Day
Literacy
6-7 Years
© A&C Black

What sank the boat?

• **Write what made the boat sink.**

1. The boat hit a _____ .
2. This made a _____
3. So _____
4. Because of this _____

_____

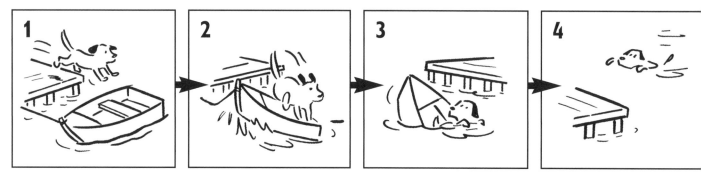

1. The dog _____
2. This made _____
3. So _____
4. Because of this _____

_____

NOW TRY THIS!

• **Find a different way to make a boat sink.**
• **Draw and write about it.**

Teachers' note Look at the first row of pictures with the children. Invite volunteers to tell the story of what happened and to say why it happened. Help them to complete the explanation. As you do so point out words and phrases supplied that help to say what made things happen: *This made, Because of this, So.*

A Lesson for Every Day
Literacy
6-7 Years
© A&C Black

What for?

- **Read the sentence starts.**
- **Choose an ending.**
- **Write** to **, then the ending.**
- **Read the longer sentence.**

Jack and Jill went up the hill to fetch a pail of water.

Old Mother Hubbard went to _____

 She went to the baker's ☐ _____

Here is a candle ☐ _____

 Here is a chopper ☐ _____

Endings

chop off your head.

to buy him some bread.

to light you to bed.

to the cupboard.

NOW TRY THIS!

- **Write new endings for these sentences.**

I ran down the road.

I turned on the tap.

Add to .

Teachers' note Revise the words the children know for joining sentences (*and, but* and *then*). Draw out in the example that Jack and Jill did two things. Ask for two sentences about these actions. Point out why *to* is useful for joining them: to show *why* Jack and Jill went up the hill. Also point out that another change had to be made and ask the children if they can spot it (*fetched* is changed to *fetch*).

A Lesson for Every Day
Literacy
6–7 Years
© A&C Black

143

- **Finish the sentences.**
- **Use** | because | .

 She put on her coat | because | _____

_____ .

 Saqib ran to school [ ] _____

_____ .

 My sister cried [ ] _____

_____ .

 Dad told us off [ ] _____

_____ .

 I had a cake with candles [ ] _____

_____ .

 Mum told us to come indoors [ ] ____

_____ .

NOW TRY THIS!

- **Answer the question. Write a sentence.**

  Why did the gingerbread man run away?

Teachers' note Remind the children of how they joined sentences in a way which showed why something was done (using *to*). Read the first example and ask them what they could write after *because*: for example, *it was cold*. Draw out that two sentences are joined to show *why*.

A Lesson for Every Day
Literacy
6–7 Years
© A&C Black

That's silly

This is silly, but it is still a sentence:

She went for a swim in the custard.

This is not silly, but it is not a sentence:

Two old men on a bench in the park.

Join these to make silly sentences.

saw a frog

in case the comb's teeth bite him.

Two old octopuses

and brushed her teeth.

Alex won't comb his hair

goes to town in a space ship.

Tina sat at the piano

were singing a merry song.

The sea bed

is where whales sleep.

My gran

driving a bus.

NOW TRY THIS!

• **Write four silly sentences starting like this.**

A can of beans   A sausage

Two rockets   The King lost his socks

Teachers' note Remind the children of their previous work on silly sentences and provide examples of silly sentences from poems or jokes for them to read aloud. Help them to pair the first example with the end of a sentence to make something silly or funny. They should draw a line to link them and then read the sentence with a friend.

A Lesson for Every Day
Literacy
6-7 Years
© A&C Black

That's the way to make it: 1

- **Look at the pictures.**
- **Make a peanut butter roll.**
- **Tell someone else how to make it.**

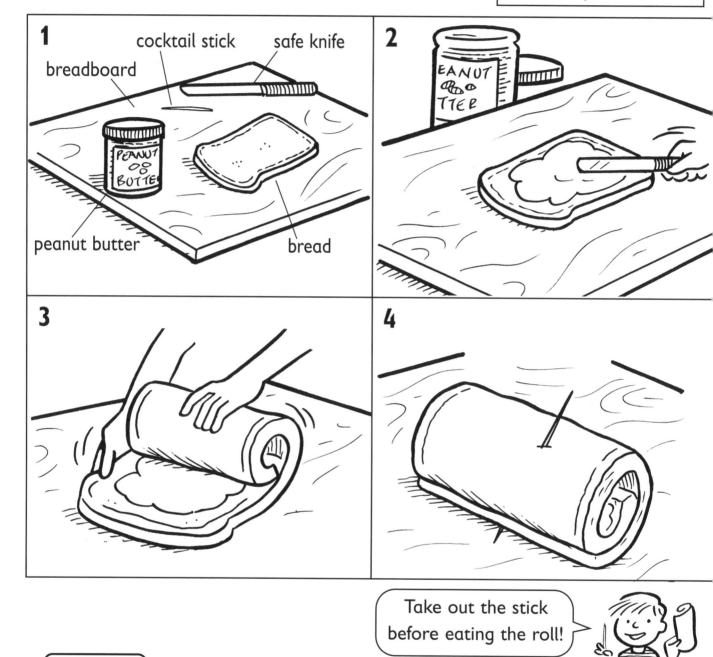

1 cocktail stick safe knife
breadboard
peanut butter bread

2 PEANUT BUTTER

3

4

Take out the stick before eating the roll!

NOW TRY THIS!

- **Show how to make the same kind of roll with another filling.**

Work with a partner.

Teachers' note If there are children with nut allergies you could replace the peanut butter with a savoury cheese spread, jam or honey. The listeners should not have carried out the activity (they could complete the one on 'That's the way to make it: 2' instead).

A Lesson for Every Day
Literacy
6-7 Years
© A&C Black

That's the way to make it: 2

- **Look at the pictures.**
- **Make some orange jellies.**
- **Tell someone else how to make them.**

1

oranges

orange jelly

water

fork

kettle

measuring jug

chopping board

lemon squeezer

sharp knife

fridge

2

⚠ Ask an adult

hot water

jelly

3

⚠ Ask an adult

orange

4

orange juice

jelly in hot water

5

jelly mixture

orange skins

fridge

NOW TRY THIS!

- **Show another group how to make a different fruit jelly.**

Teachers' note Use a packet of orange jelly dissolved in half the required amount of water. Then, if there is not enough orange juice, top it up with cold water before chilling. The jellies will need to be left for several hours or overnight to set. The listeners should not have carried out the activity (they could complete the one on 'That's the way to make it: 1' instead).

A Lesson for Every Day
Literacy
6–7 Years
© A&C Black

What am I doing?

riding a bike

eating dinner

skating

painting

writing

reading a book

playing the guitar

playing the piano

going to bed

using the computer

having a bath

walking a dog

148

A Lesson for Every Day
Literacy
6–7 Years
© A&C Black

Wordless

- **Pretend you are doing one of the actions in the stars.**
- **Your group watches and guesses which one.**

Teachers' note This could be attempted at different levels: for a less challenging activity, let the children see all the stars so that they can select the activity they think is being enacted. To make it more challenging, cut out the stars and give each one to the child who will enact the activity. Remind them to use their faces as well as hand and body actions.

A Lesson for Every Day
Literacy
6–7 Years
© A&C Black

149

Mary Seacole

- **Listen to your teacher talking about Mary Seacole.**

Work with a partner.

- **Sort the cards into three sets:**

True	Not true	Might be true

Mary Seacole was born in Jamaica.	Mary Seacole came to England in a plane.	Mary Seacole was brave.
The soldiers called Mary Seacole 'The Doctor'.	The soldiers called her 'Mother Seacole'.	Mary Seacole learned about medicine at university.
The army held a festival to raise money for Mary Seacole.	Mary Seacole got a job as a teacher.	Mary Seacole was afraid of rats.
Mary Seacole built a shop that was called 'Mrs Seacole's Hut'.	Mary Seacole made tea on the battlefields.	Mary Seacole used to drive a van onto the battlefields.

NOW TRY THIS!

- **Write two other true sentences about Mary Seacole.**
- **Give them to a partner to check.**

150

Teachers' note Tell the children that they are going to hear about Mary Seacole, who was born more than two hundred years ago. She wanted to become a nurse who looked after wounded soldiers. Remind them about 'good listening'. Read the passage in the Notes on the activities (page 18) and then cut out and sort the cards.

A Lesson for Every Day
Literacy
6–7 Years
© A&C Black

- **Listen to someone talking about a place they went to for a holiday.**
- **Write four facts about the place.**

Fact 1

Fact 2

Fact 3

Fact 4

NOW TRY THIS!

- **Ask a question about the place.**
- **Write the question and the answer.**

Teachers' note If possible, invite someone to come and talk to the children about their holiday, focusing on the location. Remind the children of 'good listening' and ask them to try to find out as much as possible about the place the speaker visited on holiday. They could make a note of four facts they learned about the place.

A Lesson for Every Day
Literacy
6-7 Years
© A&C Black

That's good

- **What does** doing good **mean?**
- **Talk to your group.**
- **Write something good to do in each flower.**

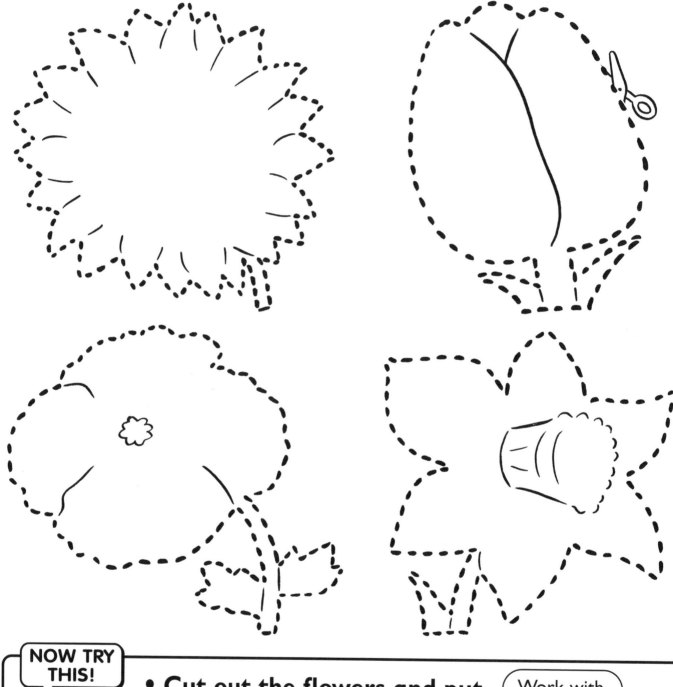

NOW TRY THIS!

- **Cut out the flowers and put them in order:**

good ──────────→ best

Work with a group.

Teachers' note Give the children time to discuss what is meant by doing good and to name some actions they think are good. Encourage children to draw on their own experiences of doing/receiving a good deed. Each member of the group can then select what they think is the most important and write it on a flower. If someone else has already chosen it they should suggest another good action.

A Lesson for Every Day
Literacy
6-7 Years
© A&C Black

That's bad

- **What are bad things to do?**
- **Talk to your group.**
- **Write something that people should not do on each bin.**

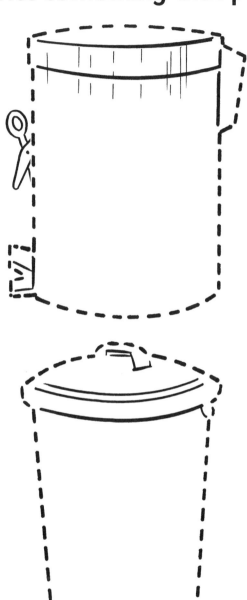

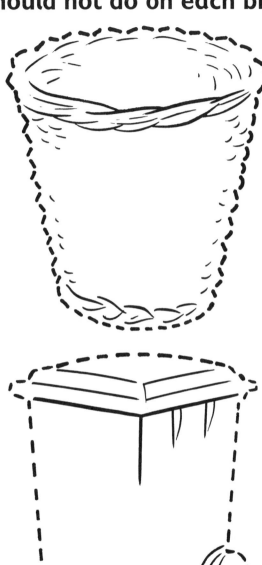

NOW TRY THIS!

- **Cut out the bins and put them in order:**

  bad ⟶ worst

Work with a group.

Teachers' note Give the children time to discuss bad actions and to name some actions they think are bad. Each member of the group can then select what they think is the most important and write it on a bin. If someone else has already chosen it they should suggest another bad action.

A Lesson for Every Day
Literacy
6-7 Years
© A&C Black

153

The chest

- **Work with a partner.**
- **What might happen when you open the chest?**
  Each write your ideas in a speech bubble.

NOW TRY THIS!

- **Act the story with your partner.
  Make it exciting.**

Teachers' note Give each child a copy of this page. Encourage the children to talk to a partner about what might be in the chest. Why are bubbles coming out of it? What might be making them? They could enact the roles of the two children in the picture. What might happen when they open the chest completely? This could lead to the development of a story.

A Lesson for Every Day
Literacy
6-7 Years
© A&C Black

Word partners

white	bull	air	tool
goal	fair	foot	gold
arm	egg	light	door
tea	hair	rail	wheel
board	dog	port	box
post	ground	ball	fish
chair	cup	house	mat
bag	clip	way	barrow

Teachers' note Show the children examples of familiar compound words, such as *teapot, teabag, handbag, bedside, doormat, goalpost, desktop, laptop, motorway*. Ask them to split these into two words and say the words. After cutting out the cards on this page they could play 'Matching pairs' or 'Find your partner'. Ask each group to list the words they make.

A Lesson for Every Day
Literacy
6-7 Years
© A&C Black

155

Oil the toy

- **Write** oi **or** oy **in the gaps.**

Example: The toy needs some oil.

R____ can j____n in our games.

Ler____ jumped for j____ when he found a c____n.

"Are you making a n____se to ann____ me?" said Miss F____.

The gardener will enj____ digging the s____l.

M____ra threw a qu____t.

The b____s were b____ling in the heat.

NOW TRY THIS!

- **Write a** rule **for spelling** oi **or** oy **words.**

Teachers' note Remind the children of the two ways of spelling the /oi/ phoneme – **oi** and **oy** – and display some words containing these phonemes: for example, *boil, coil, foil, oil, soil, toil, toilet; boy, toy.* Ask them to notice where in the word the /oi/ phoneme is and where it is spelled **oy** (at the end of a word). The grapheme **oi** is rarely seen at the end of an English word.

A Lesson for Every Day
Literacy
6-7 Years
© A&C Black

Miss Muffet's friends

- **Help Little Miss Muffet to find her friends' addresses .**
- **Which way does she need to turn the pages?**
- **Colour the arrow.**

Humpty Dumpty

L

Lucy Locket
Lost Property Office
Toytown

Georgie Porgie

D

Margery Daw
The Seesaw
Big Field
Toytown

Old King Cole

H

Little Jack Horner
2 Corner Square
Toytown

Polly Flinders

D

Yankee Doodle
8 Donkey Street
Toytown

Jenny Wren

S

Bobby Shaftoe
5 Sea Street
Toytown

Jack Sprat

H

Old Mother Hubbard
Cupboard House
Toytown

NOW TRY THIS!

- **List Little Miss Muffet's friends in alphabetical order .**

Use their last names.

Teachers' note Show the children some address books and ask them how the book is organised to help people to find addresses they have recorded. They should notice that they are in alphabetical order (usually of family name). Remind the children of their work on capital letters for names and ask them first to write the characters' names from the page showing the first letter of their second name.

A Lesson for Every Day
Literacy
6–7 Years
© A&C Black

Fairytale facts

• **Listen to the questions.**
The first to find the answer gets a counter.
The one with most counters wins.

You need

lots of counters

Character	Age	Favourite colour	Pet	Favourite food
Baby Bear	5	Green		
Giant	47	Red		
Gingerbread Man	1	Brown		
Goldilocks	7	Yellow		
Gretel	9	Blue		
Hansel	10	Purple		
Jack	11	Blue		
Red Riding Hood	8	Red		
Troll	92	White		
Witch	33	Pink		

What pet does Jack have?

What colour does Red Riding Hood like best?

How old is Hansel?

What food does Baby Bear like best?

What colour does the Troll like best?

What food does Goldilocks like best?

What pet does the Gingerbread Man have?

How old is the Giant?

What food does the Witch like best?

What pet does Gretel have?

 158

Teachers' note Begin by showing the children the class register and discussing how the names are written in order (in alphabetical order of family name). Note that most of these fairytale characters have only one name and so this register is arranged in alphabetical order of first names. Ensure the children understand that if a character likes something best, then that is his or her favourite.

A Lesson for Every Day
Literacy
6-7 Years
© A&C Black

Homes in the past web page

What did people use in the past?
- **Draw pictures for the links.**
- **Write captions.**

Web page	Link

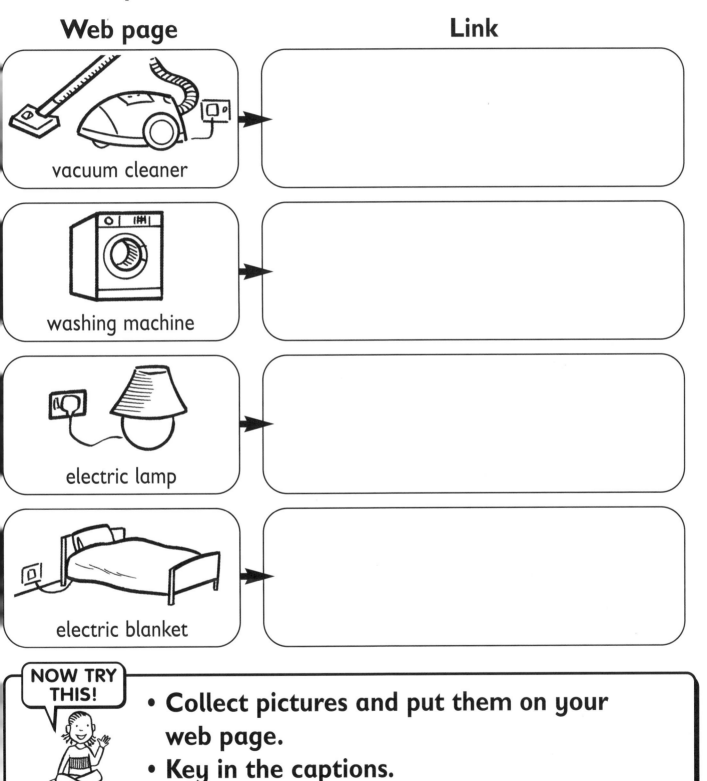

vacuum cleaner

washing machine

electric lamp

electric blanket

NOW TRY THIS!
- **Collect pictures and put them on your web page.**
- **Key in the captions.**

Teachers' note Help the children to plan a web page about homes in the past. The pictures under the heading Web page will be displayed. Each will have a link to click on to find out what was used in the past. The children's task is to find out what people in the past used instead of the items depicted and to draw or copy pictures of them and write single sentence captions for the links.

A Lesson for Every Day
Literacy
6-7 Years
© A&C Black

Toys in the past web links

How did children use these toys?
• **Write information in the links.**

Toy   **Link**

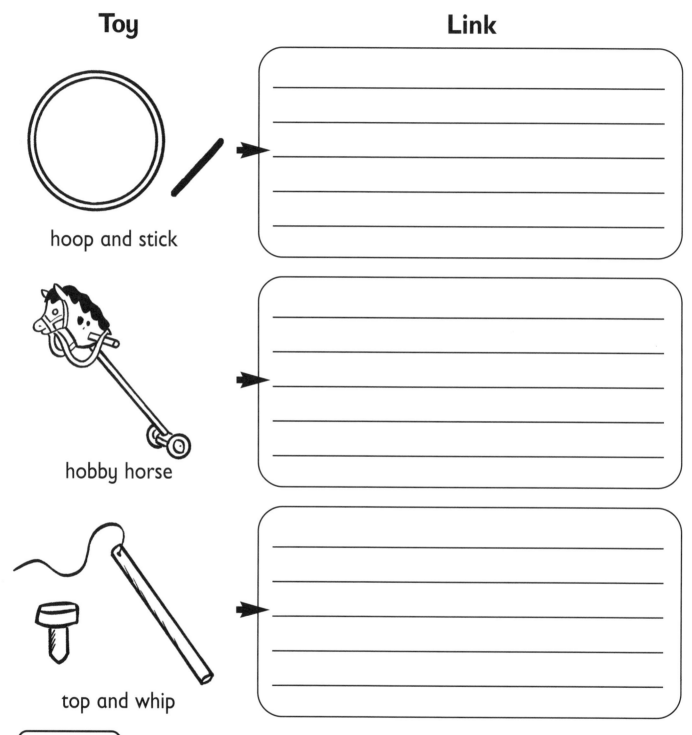

hoop and stick

hobby horse

top and whip

NOW TRY THIS!

• **Find another old toy for your web page.**
• **Key in information about it.**

Teachers' note Use this activity to help the children to plan links from a web page about toys in the past. The pictures of toys from the past will be displayed on the page. Each will have a link to click on for more information. The children's task is to find out how the toys were used and to write extended captions for the links. With help, they can then contribute to a web page about toys in the past.

A Lesson for Every Day
Literacy
6-7 Years
© A&C Black

Seaside web links

- **Find three things in the picture that we no longer use.**
- **Number them ① , ② and ③ .**
- **Write information to link to them.**

The seaside long ago

Links

① _____

_____

_____

② _____

_____

_____

③ _____

_____

_____

Teachers' note Help the children to plan links from a web page about a day at the seaside in the past. The old picture of the seaside will be displayed on the page. The numbered items will have a link to click on for more information. The children's task is to find out about them and to write information for the links. With help, they can then contribute to a web page about the seaside in the past.

A Lesson for Every Day
Literacy
6-7 Years
© A&C Black

161

Fruit: 1

apple

banana

grape

kiwi

mango

orange

peach

pear

pineapple

plum

raspberry

strawberry

Teachers' note Use this with 'Fruit: 2'. The children could first cut out the fruits, mix them up and then arrange them in alphabetical order as they would appear in a glossary. They could also colour the fruits they know and use information books, CDs or websites to find out about the colours of the others.

A Lesson for Every Day
Literacy
6-7 Years
© A&C Black

Fruit: 2

- **Find out about four fruits.**
- **Write notes on the chart.**

Small seeds?

How many?

Pips?

Stone?

Vine?

Small plant?

Bush?

Tree?

Fruit	Colour	Size	Type of plant	Seeds

NOW TRY THIS!

- **Write a sentence about each fruit.**

Teachers' note Use this with 'Fruit: 1'. The children choose four fruits to research using information texts. They write notes based on the hints in the speech bubbles. Later they could use their notes to help them to write their own information page about a fruit. Different children could focus on different fruits to contribute to a class information book about fruit.

A Lesson for Every Day
Literacy
6–7 Years
© A&C Black

- **Plan an information book about fruit.**

Make chapters about fruits with stones, pips or seeds.

Make a page about each fruit.

Chapter 1	Fruits with a stone
Page	Heading
1	Mangos
2	_____
_____	_____
Chapter 2	Fruits with _____
_____	_____
_____	_____
_____	_____
_____	_____
Chapter 3	_____
_____	_____
_____	_____
_____	_____
_____	_____
_____	_____

Teachers' note See 'Fruit: 1 and 2'. The children should first have looked at how simple information books are organised – unlike fiction, not according to events. How does this contents page group the fruits into chapters? Ask the children to use the information they have collected to help them to put the fruits in the correct chapters.

A Lesson for Every Day
Literacy
6–7 Years
© A&C Black

But

- **Read the sentences.**
- **Join each sentence to an ending.**
- **Write** but **on the line.**
- **Read the long sentences.**

I like apples and bananas	*but*	it starts first time every day.
Ella can run fast		he came last in the high jump.
Jay won the long jump		I don't like grapes.
This soup is too hot		Mum likes France better.
My Dad wants to go to Spain		she can't swim.
Our car is very old		that one is too cold.

NOW TRY THIS!

- **Make these sentences longer.**

  I like playing football

  Dan's house is very big

  Amy has a big brown dog

Add but .

Teachers' note Explain that we can join two sentences to make one long sentence: one way of doing this is to put in a word which makes sense, such as *and* or *but*. Remind the children how *and* is used: *I came home and I played with Ella.* Point out that sentences can be joined with *but* if you want to show a difference. Read the completed example with them and discuss why *but* is used.

A Lesson for Every Day
Literacy
6–7 Years
© A&C Black

Then

- **Read the sentence beginnings.**
- **Join each beginning to an ending.**
- **Draw a line.**
- **Write** | then | **on the line.**
- **Read the long sentence.**

| She ate a cake |
| We saw a flash of light |
| He put on his coat |
| A big black cloud came |
| The car stopped |

then

| it began to rain. |
| went out for a walk. |
| a man got out. |
| heard a loud bang. |
| drank some tea. |

NOW TRY THIS!

Add | then |.

- **Make these sentences longer.**

He put a stamp on the letter

I came home from school

Teachers' note Remind the children of the words they know for joining sentences (*and* and *but*).
Read the example and point out why *then* is useful for joining these sentences: it shows that one thing
happens *after* the other. Discuss: *I came home and I played with Ella.* Draw out that *then* could be
used instead of *and*. This would stress that one thing happened *after* the other.

A Lesson for Every Day
Literacy
6–7 Years
© A&C Black

Tell me when

- **Read what they say.**
- **Fill in the gaps.**
- **Then write the sentences.**

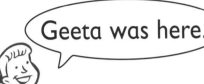 Geeta was here. When? Yesterday.

Geeta was here
_____

I went to Florida. When? Last year.

I went
_____

We met the Queen. When? On Friday.

_____

 There was a storm. When? At 2 o'clock.

_____

NOW TRY THIS!
- **Write sentences about these times.**
  - when you were five
  - when you last went swimming
  - when the weather was cold

Teachers' note Review the children's previous learning about the different parts of a sentence by reminding them of one of the questions they were asked: *When? Where?* Invite volunteers to give sentences saying when they did things such as brushing their teeth, going swimming, eating lunch. They can then use the question prompt to help them to complete each sentence.

A Lesson for Every Day
Literacy
6-7 Years
© A&C Black

Question time

You can turn a [sentence] **into a** [question] .

[Sentence] It is raining today.

[Question] Is it raining today?

- **Turn these sentences into questions.**

1 This is Ali's bike.

2 May can skip fast.

3 He has a new phone.

4 His dogs are corgis.

5 We can go to the party.

6 She will win the race.

1 _____

2 _____

3 _____

4 _____

5 _____

6 _____

NOW TRY THIS!

- **Turn these sentences into questions.**

  He knows the answer.

  They are playing chess.

Teachers' note How can you tell if a question is a sentence, even if there is no question mark? Draw out that they can start with a question word or words can be turned around: *it is/is it, she has/has she.* Write up a sentence for the children to make into a question by changing the positions of two words: for example, *He is going home.* Remind them to change the full stop to a question mark.

A Lesson for Every Day
Literacy
6-7 Years
© A&C Black

The comma

This is a **comma** **,** .

You can put a comma after each part of a list.

In my pocket I have a conker, a sweet, a mouse and some sawdust.

You don't need a comma before **and** .

• Put the commas in the sentences.

1 At the party I saw Leo Tom Bella and Sunita.

2 Each wizard had a wand an owl a cat and a broomstick.

3 We played football cricket rounders and tennis.

4 The playground had a slide swings a roundabout a seesaw and a climbing frame.

5 Along the road we found a beech tree two oaks a lime and a rowan.

6 My gran gave me a pound some felt-tips a pen and a ruler.

Remember – no comma before **and** .

NOW TRY THIS!

• Write a sentence to list your favourite toys.
• Put a comma after each part of the list.

Teachers' note Show examples of vertically listed items, such as shopping lists. Draw out that they are not written as sentences. Explain that a list can be part of a sentence. Read the first example and draw out how the commas are used to separate the items. Write up the same sentence without commas and read it aloud. Emphasise the way in which the words run into one another without a pause.

A Lesson for Every Day
Literacy
6-7 Years
© A&C Black

Play the game

- **Read the instructions for playing 'Lucy Locket'.**
- **Play the game.**
- **Tell another group how to play.**

Play in a group of six.

Lucy Locket lost her pocket, Kitty Fisher found it…

Choose someone to start. They skip round the circle. They carry a small bag.

There was not a penny in it, just a ribbon round it…

The person skipping drops the bag behind someone.

This person picks up the bag and skips round the circle… then drops the bag behind someone.

This one picks up the bag and skips round the circle…

NOW TRY THIS!

- **What if two children lose their pockets?**
- **Talk to a partner about how to change the game.**

Teachers' note Explain that when this rhyme was written a 'pocket' was a cloth or leather bag fastened with a ribbon or cord, stitched into their clothing. Adapt this so that the child skipping round the outside of the circle continues while the others repeat 'Round it, round it…' until he or she drops the pocket. The child skipping has to listen to the singing to know when to drop the pocket.

A Lesson for Every Day
Literacy
6-7 Years
© A&C Black

Play the game questions

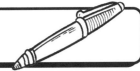

- **Answer the questions about 'Lucy Locket'.**
- **Write in the speech bubbles.**

How do you choose who will start?

_____
_____
_____

Which way do they skip round the circle?

_____
_____
_____

How do they choose the next person?

_____
_____
_____

Where does the first skipper go when the next one begins?

_____
_____
_____

- **Write another question.**
- **Ask a partner to answer it.**

Teachers' note Use this with 'Play the game'. The children who read the instructions can answer the questions to check their understanding of the instructions and those whom they tell how to play the game could then answer them too. These questions can also be used to help the children to devise their own 'circle' game (see 'A new game', page 172).

A Lesson for Every Day
Literacy
6–7 Years
© A&C Black

A new game

- **Make up a new 'circle' game like 'Lucy Locket'.**
- **Write instructions.**
- **Tell your group how to play.**

Name of game _____

Words	Actions
1	1
2	2
3	3

I lost my dog.

I lost my bone.

NOW TRY THIS!

- **Think of a way to end the game.**
- **Talk to your group about it.**
- **Try your idea.**

Teachers' note Discuss the format of 'circle' games and ask the children about the roles of the different players. The questions on 'Play the game questions' can be used to help them to devise a new game. This could be linked with a PE lesson in which they can try out their games and modify the rules as necessary.

A Lesson for Every Day
Literacy
6-7 Years
© A&C Black

In the groove

love	glove	grove	drove
shove	dove	stove	cove
move	groove	drive	dive
give	active	five	alive
arrive	hive	slave	brave
grave	shave	sleeve	weave
leave	believe	serve	curve
carve	starve	solve	revolve

Teachers' note Read a list of words ending with the /**v**/ phoneme and not on this page: for example, cave, gave, have, save, wave, heave, leave. Ask the children to write the words on a wipe-off board. Invite them to display their words and ask them which letter they end with. They could play 'Matching pairs' or 'Find your partner' with the cards, according to the sound before the /**v**/ phoneme.

A Lesson for Every Day
Literacy
6-7 Years
© **A&C Black**

173

Worker words

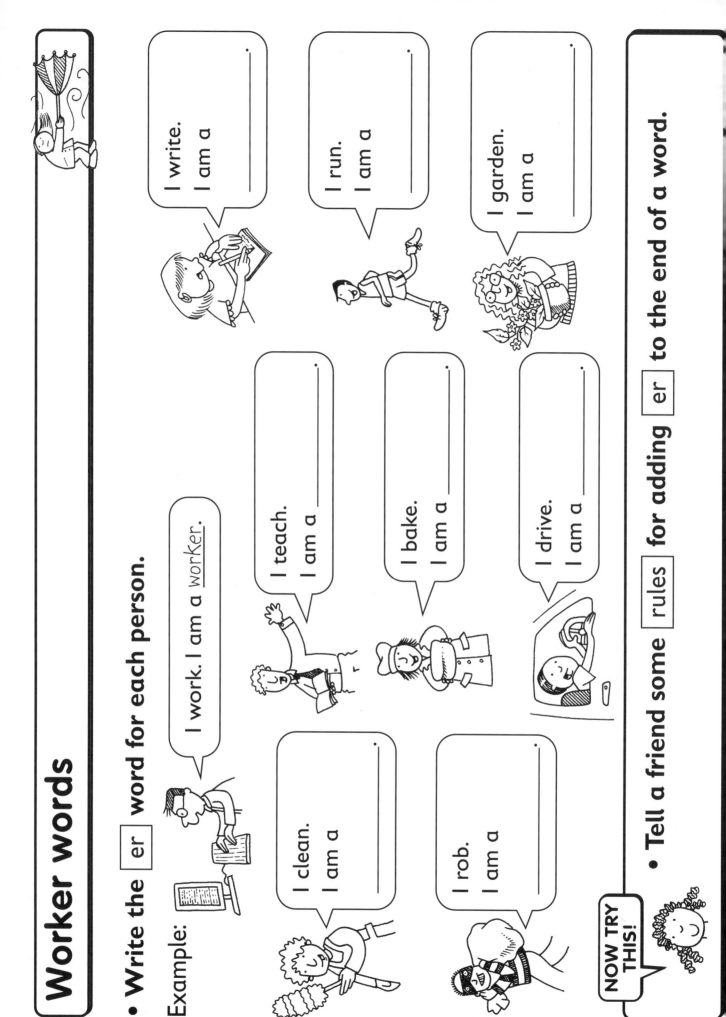

- **Write the** `er` **word for each person.**

Example:

I work. I am a <u>worker</u>.

I write. I am a _____.

I run. I am a _____.

I garden. I am a _____.

I teach. I am a _____.

I bake. I am a _____.

I drive. I am a _____.

I clean. I am a _____.

I rob. I am a _____.

NOW TRY THIS!

- **Tell a friend some** `rules` **for adding** `er` **to the end of a word.**

Teachers' note Begin by saying *I teach. I am a teacher. You learn. You are learners.* Continue with other examples for the children to complete: *X plays football. He is a footballer. Y farms. She is a farmer.* Write up the base words and invite the children to add the **-er** suffix. Introduce examples where the final **e** of the base word is dropped or the final consonant doubled: *rider; winner.*

A Lesson for Every Day
Literacy
6-7 Years
© A&C Black

Island reports

- **Find out about an island.**

You need these texts

a travel brochure

a book

a website

Name of island _____

- **Skim the texts.**
- **What will they tell you?** ✔
- **Check:**

contents | menu | headings | site map | index | illustrations

| Text | What it tells us ✔ | | | | | |
	Where the island is	Which sea it is in	How big it is	What the land is like	What people have built	What work they do there
Travel brochure						
Book						
Website						

NOW TRY THIS!

- **Write three questions about the island.**
- **Make sure you know the answers!**

Teachers' note This page could be linked with work in geography on an island home. Remind the children that they do not need to read the leaflet and book from cover to cover and that they need not read every word on the website (see the notes on the activity on page 20). Also remind them how to scan these information texts in order to find the information they want.

A Lesson for Every Day
Literacy
6-7 Years
© A&C Black

Island fact-file

- **Find out about an island.**
- **Use the Internet.**
- **Check:** | menu | | site map | | links | | photos | | maps |
- **Record what you found out.**

	Island	
Size	**Where it is**	

Landscape ☑

| moorland ☐ | hills ☐ | forests ☐ |
| farmland ☐ | lakes ☐ | rivers ☐ |

Coast ☑

| beaches ☐ | cliffs ☐ | bays ☐ |
| sand dunes ☐ | rocks ☐ | marshes ☐ |

Buildings ☑

houses ☐	shops ☐	factories ☐
churches ☐	other places of worship ☐	
post offices ☐	banks ☐	garages ☐

NOW TRY THIS!

- **Write a question about a building on the island.**
- **Give it to a friend to find the answer.**

Teachers' note This follows on from 'Island reports'. Once the children have located the type of information they want, encourage them to find out about a specific aspect of the island – the land and what has been built on it. Once they have recorded the facts you could also ask them to construct sentences about the natural and built features of the island.

A Lesson for Every Day
Literacy
6-7 Years
© A&C Black

Note it

Meera has made notes about materials she saw in the street.

Meera

Use my notes to write sentences.

Material	Used for	Why
stone	kerb	t
wood	door	h
plastic	bags	b
metal	grid	s
glass	window	tr

Glass is used for windows because it is _____.

This material is strong: _____.

Stone is used for kerbs because it is _____.

Wood is used for doors because it is _____.

Plastic is used for bags because it is _____.

Teachers' note Explain that making notes means recording information in a quick way and that one way of doing this is to use a chart with headings. Tell the children that once they have made a note of all the information they need. They can then write about it in sentences.

A Lesson for Every Day
Literacy
6-7 Years
© A&C Black

Double page plan

- Plan two pages of a book.
- Where will you put these?
- Write in the boxes.

heading | sub-heading | picture | caption | information

2

3

Dinosaur report

Cut out the pieces of a report.

Sort them out: | introduction | | two chapters |

Write sub-headings.

Stegosaurus means *roof lizard*. Its length was up to 9 metres. It ate plants. It has been found in the USA.

Diplodocus means *double beam*. Its length was up to 26 metres. It ate plants. It has been found in the USA.

Tyrannosaurus means *tyrant lizard*. Its length was up to 12 metres. It ate other animals. It could open its mouth to one metre high. It has been found in the USA.

Bactrosaurus means *club-spined lizard*. Its length was up to 6 metres. It ate plants. It has been found in Mongolia in Asia.

Triceratops means *three-horned face*. Its length was up to 9 metres. It ate plants. It has been found in the USA.

Allosaurus means *other lizard*. Its length was up to 12 metres. It ate other animals. It has been found in the USA and in Tanzania in Africa.

Dinosaur means *fearsome lizard*. Dinosaurs were different kinds of reptiles that lived on the earth from about 230 million years ago. Some of them ate plants; others ate other animals. They died out about 65 million years ago. Scientists are not sure why they died out.

An allosaurus | A triceratops

A bactrosaurus

A stegosaurus

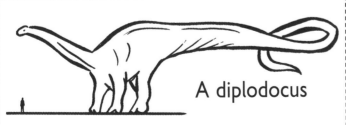

A diplodocus

A tyrannosaurus

Teachers' note Working in pairs or small groups, the children take turns to read part of the report aloud. Which is the introduction? After the introduction, the report has two chapters – each about a group of dinosaurs. Can they find the clue in the introduction that tells them what the two groups are? (meat-eaters and plant-eaters)

A Lesson for Every Day
Literacy
6–7 Years
© A&C Black

Habitats plan

What do you know about habitats in your school grounds?

- Write on the idea map.

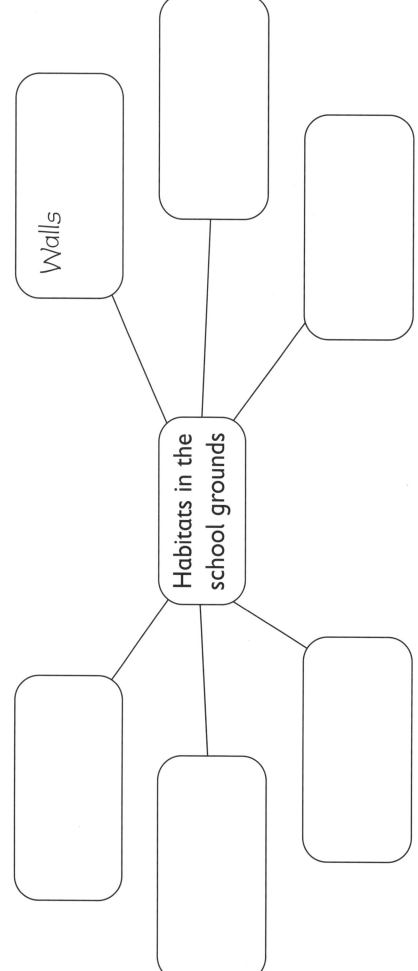

Walls

Habitats in the
school grounds

Write everything
you know about it.

A Lesson for Every Day
Literacy
6–7 Years
© A&C Black

NOW TRY THIS!

- **Choose a habitat.**
- **Write notes about it.**

Teachers' note Use this page to help the children to prepare for finding out about habitats in the school grounds (or another local site). Invite feedback and encourage the children to write questions to help them find out more in order to write a non-chronological report. See also 'Two habitats', page 181.

Two habitats

• **Write notes about two habitats.**

Habitat _____

What it is like _____

_____

_____

Plants that grow there _____

_____

Animals that visit or live there _____

_____

Habitat _____

What it is like _____

_____

_____

Plants that grow there _____

_____

Animals that visit or live there _____

_____

NOW TRY THIS!

• **Write sentences from your notes about a habitat.**

Use sub-headings.

Teachers' note See 'Habitats plan'. These pages can be used in connection with work in science. They can use this page for recording what they find out about habitats in the school grounds or another local place. Remind them how to write notes – omitting unimportant words, shortening words and using the figures for numbers instead of the words.

A Lesson for Every Day
Literacy
6-7 Years
© A&C Black

Paragraphs

Make a mark like this where each new paragraph should start: |

There are different kinds of fairies. Some are good. Some are mischievous. Others are evil. True fairies are good. They are very tiny, can fly and do magic. Brownies are Scottish fairies. They are very tiny and live in our houses. Brownies are good. They help around the house but they do not like to be seen, so they only work at night. People give them presents of food and they love porridge. If anyone is cruel to a Brownie it turns into a Boggart. A Boggart is an evil spirit that makes things disappear. It turns the milk sour, and makes dogs lame. Families move house to get away from a Boggart but the Boggart follows them. Most Goblins live in woods. They play tricks on people. They can be any size, from very tiny up to human size. Gnomes are like Goblins but they are all very tiny. Pixies are very tiny fairies who play tricks on people. They steal or hide their things or throw things at them. They steal horses at night and bring them back before morning with tangled manes. They leave Pixie dust in their footprints and in the air as they fly. Trolls are very ugly and evil and live in caves. Most trolls are the size of humans, but some are giants.

NOW TRY THIS!

- **Find out about another type of fairy.**
- **Write a paragraph about them.**

Teachers' note Read this non-chronological report together and point out how the first sentence introduces the topic. How could this report be split into paragraphs? They could reread it with a friend, stopping where they think a new paragraph should start. Display it on screen so that they can use the Return key to create new paragraphs.

A Lesson for Every Day
Literacy
6–7 Years
© A&C Black

A poem to read aloud: 1

- **Read the poem silently.**
- **Underline the FAST lines in red.**
- **Underline the SLOW lines in blue.**
- **Read the poem aloud to a partner.**

Work with a partner.

A lazy thought

There go the grown-ups
To the office,
To the store.
Subway rush,
Traffic crush;
Hurry, scurry,
Worry, flurry.

No wonder
Grown-ups
Don't grow up
Any more.

It takes a lot
Of slow
To grow.   Eve Merriam

NOW TRY THIS!

- **Write some other words about hurrying.**
- **Say them so that they sound like their meanings.**
- **Write some other words about going slowly.**
- **Say them so that they sound like their meanings.**

Teachers' note After the children have read and marked the poem, invite volunteers to read it to the group or class. Discuss any differences in speed and let the children decide on the most appropriate way of reading the poem.

A Lesson for Every Day
Literacy
6-7 Years
© A&C Black

183

A poem to read aloud: 2

- **Read the poem with a partner.**
- **One of you reads the questions.**
- **The other reads the answers.**

Make your voice sound like a question or answer.

O Dandelion

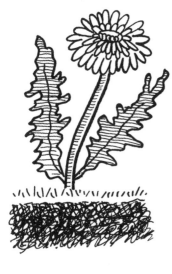

'O dandelion, yellow as gold,
What do you do all day?'

'I just wait here in the tall green grass
Till the children come to play.'

'O dandelion, yellow as gold,
What do you do all night?'

'I wait and wait till the cool dews fall
And my hair grows long and white.'

'And what do you do when your hair is white,
And the children come to play?'

'They take me up in their dimpled hands
And blow my hair away!'

Anonymous

NOW TRY THIS!

- **Write a question to ask another flower.**
- **Write the answer.**
- **Read them aloud with a partner.**

Teachers' note Begin by reading the poem aloud with no expression – the questions in the same tone of voice as the answers. Ask the children to comment on how you read it. They can then try making the questions sound like questions and the answers sound like statements.

A Lesson for Every Day
Literacy
6-7 Years
© A&C Black

Laughometer

- **Tell your group a joke.**
- **How much did they laugh?**
- **Record it on the laughometer.**

1	**2**
What breakfast cereal do cats eat? Mice crispies.	"Doctor, doctor – I keep thinking I'm a pair of curtains." "You'll just have to pull yourself together."
3	**4**
"Doctor, doctor – I keep thinking I'm invisible." "Who said that?"	Teacher: Wayne, why have you not given me your homework? Wayne: I made it into a paper aeroplane and someone hijacked it.

Laughometer

Joke	How much they laughed			
	☹	😐	☺	😄
1				
2				
3				
4				

NOW TRY THIS!

- **Find another joke.**
- **Tell it to different people in different ways.**
- **Record how much they laughed.**

Use a laughometer.

Teachers' note Cut out the jokes and give the children one each to read in groups of four or make four different copies of the page, each with all but one joke masked (a different joke each time). Use these pages as master copies to make a set for each group. The children should read only their own joke.

A Lesson for Every Day
Literacy
6-7 Years
© A&C Black

185

Cold hands

- **Ms Carr's hands get very cold in the playground.**
- **What kind of gloves will be the best?**
- **Take a vote:** ✔

Cotton gloves			
Sheepskin gloves			
Fleece gloves			
Woollen gloves			

- **Which gloves does your group think will be the best?**

_____

- **Plan how to find out.**
- **Decide what you each will do.**
- **Draw and write your plan.**

Names	What they will do	What we shall do

Teachers' note Ask the children to share their ideas about the kind of gloves that will keep the teacher's hands the warmest, and why. They can then discuss how to find out and go on to plan an investigation, allocating the tasks among the group.

A Lesson for Every Day
Literacy
6-7 Years
© A&C Black

The Jolly Hunter

- Read the poem with a partner.
- Say what you think about it.

I Saw a Jolly Hunter

I saw a jolly hunter
With a jolly gun
Walking in the country
In the jolly sun.

In the jolly meadow
Sat a jolly hare.
Saw the jolly hunter.
Took jolly care.

Hunter jolly eager –
Sight of jolly prey.
Forgot gun pointing
Wrong jolly way.

Jolly hunter jolly head
Over heels gone.
Jolly old safety-catch
Not jolly on.

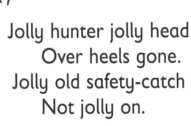

Bang!

Bang went the jolly gun.
Hunter jolly dead.
Hare got clean away,
Jolly good, I said.

Charles Causley

NOW TRY THIS!

- Tell another pair what you said.
- Ask what they said.
- Check that everyone in your group has had a chance to speak.

Teachers' note Mask all but the first verse of the poem. After reading it, the children should say what kind of poem they think it will be. Which words make them think that? Let them read the second verse and say if they still think the same, then the third verse and so on. Talk about what the poem says about hunting. Does the poet care more about the hare or the hunter?

A Lesson for Every Day
Literacy
6-7 Years
© A&C Black

On stage

- **Watch a play.**
  What was it like? ✔ **or** ✘

exciting

lively

funny

- **How did the music and lights help to make it feel like this? Fill in the chart.**

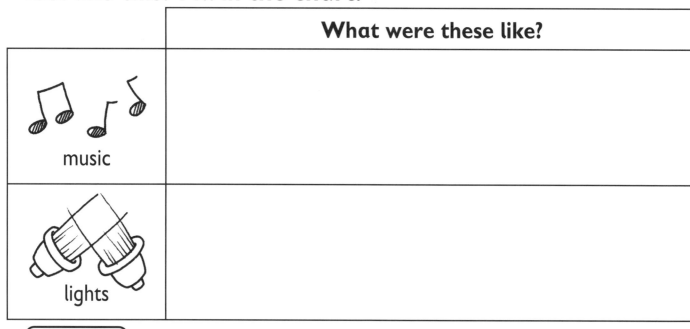

	What were these like?
♪ music	
lights	

NOW TRY THIS!

- **What else made it feel like this? Talk to a partner. Describe two of the things you saw or heard.**

Teachers' note Use this activity after the children have watched a play. Discuss how they responded to it. Did they laugh at some parts? Did any parts make them feel sad? If so, which parts, and why? Model a response to suspense (gasping or clapping a hand to your mouth and widening your eyes). Did the children feel like this at times? How did the music or lights help to create these feelings?

A Lesson for Every Day
Literacy
6-7 Years
© A&C Black

Sea song

- **Read the poem aloud.**
- **Say the missing words.**
- **Write the missing words.**

Sea song

Sea-shell, sea-shell,
Murmuring sand,
Murmuring sand.

Sea-shell, sea-shell,
Far-away land,

_____.

_____,

Sing in my hand,

_____.

_____,

I'll understand,
You'll _____.

James Kirkup

NOW TRY THIS!

- **Make up another verse.**
- **Choose from these words.**

band, grand, stand

Teachers' note Read the first verse of the poem aloud, then begin the second verse; stop after land. If the children cannot continue, point out the pattern of the first verse (the second line is repeated). Reread the second verse and let the children complete the missing part orally. Ask them to talk to a friend about the missing lines in the third verse. Point out that the fourth verse is slightly different.

A Lesson for Every Day
Literacy
6–7 Years
© A&C Black

189

Shoe chant

- **Continue the chant.**
- **Write in the speech bubbles.**

Use the rhyme-bank.
Count the beats.

 White shoes.   Bright shoes.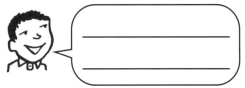

 Pinch your toes so tight shoes.

 _____ _____

 _____

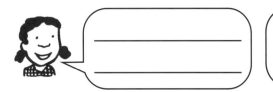 _____ _____

_____

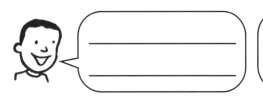 _____ _____

 _____

Rhyme-bank

grey   play
run away

new   blue
worn by
you-know-who

old   gold
fancy
rubber-soled

strappy   tappy
make you feel
so happy

green   clean
best you've
ever seen

brown   town
turned-up for
a clown

NOW TRY THIS!

- **Chant the poem with a friend.**
- **Mark any parts you want to change.**

190

Teachers' note This chant is based on the rhythm of 'Bug Chant' by Tony Mitton which the children should hear first. Encourage them to join in a reading of the chant, emphasising the rhythm. They should notice the rhyme pattern and use the sets of three rhyming words for each verse: for example, *Grey shoes. Play shoes. Make you run away shoes.*

A Lesson for Every Day
Literacy
6-7 Years
© A&C Black

Sentence link

- **Make long sentences.**
- **Write** and , but , then , because **or** to .

1 We went to town ⬚ buy some shoes.

2 He bent down ⬚ picked up a coin.

3 She can sing ⬚ she can't dance.

4 We couldn't play football ⬚ the pitch was flooded.

5 They ran to the corner ⬚ looked for Milly.

6 Rosie could see the moon ⬚ she couldn't see any stars.

7 The little boy cried ⬚ he was lost.

8 Mum gave me some money ⬚ buy a book.

NOW TRY THIS!

- **Write five long sentences.**
- **Use these words in them.**

and but then because to

Teachers' note Remind the children of the words they know for joining sentences (*and, but, then, because* and *to*). Read the example and ask the children to try different words in the gap. Discuss which is best, and why. They could then read the sentences with a friend and discuss which word would make the best sense in each gap.

A Lesson for Every Day
Literacy
6-7 Years
© A&C Black

Sentence robots

Help the robots to make sentences.

- **Circle a set of words from each robot.**
- **Write the sentences.**

A rocket

Two logs

A spider

rolled

crept

zoomed

into space.

over the step.

down the hill.

A snail

An elephant

An owl

flew

slid

crashed

across the sky.

through the trees.

along the wall.

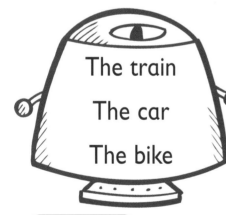

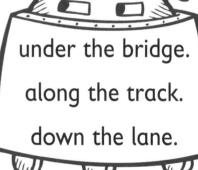

The train

The car

The bike

sped

rattled

chugged

under the bridge.

along the track.

down the lane.

NOW TRY THIS!

- **Make three sentences from the robots' words.**
- **Add another word to make longer sentences.**

Teachers' note Tell the children that they are going to choose a word or set of words from each robot to make a sentence reading across the page. They could make this either silly or sensible. Ask them questions about the sentence: *Who? What did it do? Where?*

A Lesson for Every Day
Literacy
6-7 Years
© A&C Black

Loud and quiet

- **Read the story to yourself.**
- **Underline parts to read quietly in** `green` **.**
- **Underline parts to read loudly in** `red` **.**
- **Then read the story aloud.**

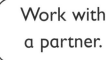

Work with a partner.

"Goodnight, Aunt Sophia. Goodnight Uncle Simon," called Gregg, as he got into bed. They were watching TV.

"G'nigh," growled Uncle Simon.

"'Night," came Aunt Sophia's shrill voice.

Gregg looked at the locked door at the end of the landing.

He tiptoed along the landing. He stopped and listened. Nothing.
Just the faint sound of a football match on TV downstairs.
He tried the doorknob. It was locked. He put his ear to the door.
Nothing, then…

"Aaaah! No!"

The voice came from behind the locked door. Gregg ran softly to his bedroom.

NOW TRY THIS!

- **Write the rest of the story.**
- **Read your story aloud with a partner.**

Teachers' note Begin by reading the story aloud in a monotonous way and then ask the children what was wrong with the way in which you read it. Ask them how you could make it sound more interesting: for example, by changing your voice for different characters. Point out that some parts should be read more quietly than others.

A Lesson for Every Day
Literacy
6–7 Years
© A&C Black

On wheels: the vehicles

small saloon car

Formula 1 car

transit van

motorbike

people carrier

landrover

Teachers' note Use this with page 195. Introduce the term vehicle. The children could say what they know about each type of vehicle and how it is useful. With help, they could find out more from manufacturers' leaflets or websites.

A Lesson for Every Day
Literacy
6-7 Years
© A&C Black

On wheels: the drivers

- **Choose a vehicle for one of these drivers.**
- **Say what makes it the best.**

Work with a group.

Jane the farmer

Simon the racing driver

Ella the electrician

Ben the scrap-metal dealer

Ali the learner driver

Rose, who has six children

Driver	Vehicle

Each say something about your choice.

Why we chose this vehicle

_____

_____

_____

_____

_____

_____

_____

_____

NOW TRY THIS!

- **Choose some materials for making a model of the vehicle.**

Teachers' note The children should first have discussed the vehicles on 'On wheels: the vehicles'. They should consider each driver in turn and say what this person might use the vehicle for and what they think he or she needs in a vehicle.

A Lesson for Every Day
Literacy
6–7 Years
© A&C Black

Setting the scene

- ## Work with a group.
- ## Plan the opening scene for a video.
  ## It could be:

Title	Type of video

Setting

Lights

Music

NOW TRY THIS!

- ## Try your ideas.
  ## Make changes if you need to.

Teachers' note You could begin by showing the children the opening scene of a film or television programme and asking them what kind of film/programme they think it will be (for example, funny, exciting, romantic, scary) and how they can tell. Focus on the setting, lighting and music and their effects. If possible, provide CDs, torches, paints and so on for the children to try out their ideas.

A Lesson for Every Day
Literacy
6-7 Years
© A&C Black

Quiet poems: 1

- **Listen to the poem.**
- **What can you hear if you lie in bed very still and very quiet?**
- **Talk to a friend about these sounds.**
- **Write them on the notepad.**

Work with a friend.

Night Sounds

When I lie in bed
I think I can hear
The stars being switched on
I think I can.

And I think I can hear
The moon
Breathing.

But I have to be still.
So still.
All the house is sleeping.
Except for me.

Then I think I can hear it.

Berlie Doherty

Notepad

the birds snoring

_____

_____

_____

_____

_____

_____

_____

_____

_____

NOW TRY THIS!

- **Complete the verse with your own words.**

  When I lie in bed
  I think I can hear

  _____

  _____

Teachers' note Have the children sitting very still and quiet and, if possible, darken the room slightly. If you have time you could pin up a few stars and a moon before you begin. Read the poem softly and discuss it in hushed voices: ask the children what quiet things they think they can hear at night. You might need to suggest some: for example, the sky turning over, an owl blinking.

A Lesson for Every Day
Literacy
6-7 Years
© A&C Black

Quiet poems: 2

- **Read the poem to yourself.**
- **How will you read it aloud?**
- **What actions will you do?**
- **Write notes in the boxes.**

Shhhhhhhh!

How to read

<u>in a whisper</u>

Listen

Shhhhhhhhh!

Sit still, very still

And listen.

Listen to wings

Lighter than eyelashes

Stroking the air.

Know what the thin breeze

Whispers on high

To the coconut trees.

Listen and hear.

Telcine Turner

Actions

<u>put my finger to</u>
<u>my lips</u>

NOW TRY THIS!

- **Write six words that sound quiet.**
- **Use some of these to help you to write a line for a quiet poem.**

Teachers' note The children should first have read some quiet poems or completed 'Quiet poems: 1'.
Ask them to read it to themselves and to think about how they will read it aloud, then ask them to read
it in unison (this could be carried out in small groups at different times). Ask them which parts told
them it should be read quietly. They could underline these.

A Lesson for Every Day
Literacy
6–7 Years
© A&C Black

Words and pictures

- **Match the words to the pictures.**
- **Write them on the lines.**

dee dum, dee dum dum, dum, dum	tip-toe, tip-toe stop – listen

Whoosh! Whizz! Stars scream	Chattering wheels Rushing along

_____

_____

_____

_____

- **Draw a picture of something you have watched.**
- **Write some words for the sounds.**

Teachers' note Before giving out copies of this sheet, invite four volunteers to read the four sets of words aloud to the class. Ask the other children if that is how they would read them. Remind them of rhymes/songs that use these effects: for example, *I hear thunder...; Horsey horsey, don't you stop...* Ask them what pictures they see in their minds when they hear the words.

A Lesson for Every Day
Literacy
6–7 Years
© A&C Black

Rough or smooth

- **Read the words aloud.**
- **Listen to the** | sounds |**.**
- **Write them in the shapes.**

Do the words sound rough or smooth?

cool	gravel	pillow	rocky
cracker	harsh	prickle	roll
fleece	jagged	puff	snatch
flower	lullaby	rattle	velvet

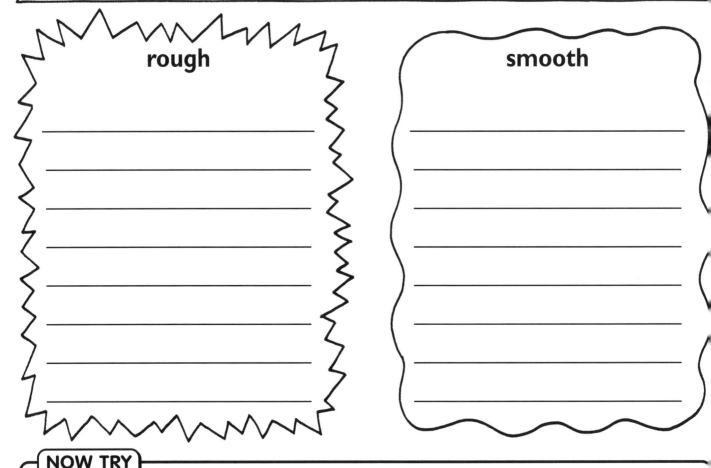

rough

smooth

NOW TRY THIS!

- **Write two more** | rough | **words.**
- **Write two more** | smooth | **words.**

Teachers' note Explain that you are going to say a word and that the children should decide if it sounds rough or smooth. (Say *rough* in a rough way and *smooth* in a smooth way.) It doesn't matter whether or not they know the words. Say a few more words for extra practice: *gruff, melody, scratchy, scrape, seamless.* Why is there sometimes a connection between the sound of a word and its meaning?

A Lesson for Every Day
Literacy
6–7 Years
© A&C Black

Caterpillar

- Choose words that say
  - what a caterpillar looks like
  - what it feels like
  - how it moves.

- **Write them on the caterpillar.**

Word-bank

bristles	jumps	slimy
bumpy	long	slippery
coils	munches	soft
curls	puffy	springy
fat	runs	squeezes
hairy	silent	stiff
hops	slides	tickles
humps	slowly	walks

NOW TRY THIS!

- Write three lines for a poem about a caterpillar.

Teachers' note Let the children observe some caterpillars closely. Do not let them touch them. Ask them to decide which words in the word-bank are good for showing how they move or for describing them. They could cross out the words they will not use. Set a limit on the number of words they can write on the caterpillar to encourage them to choose carefully.

A Lesson for Every Day
Literacy
6–7 Years
© A&C Black

201

Cat watch

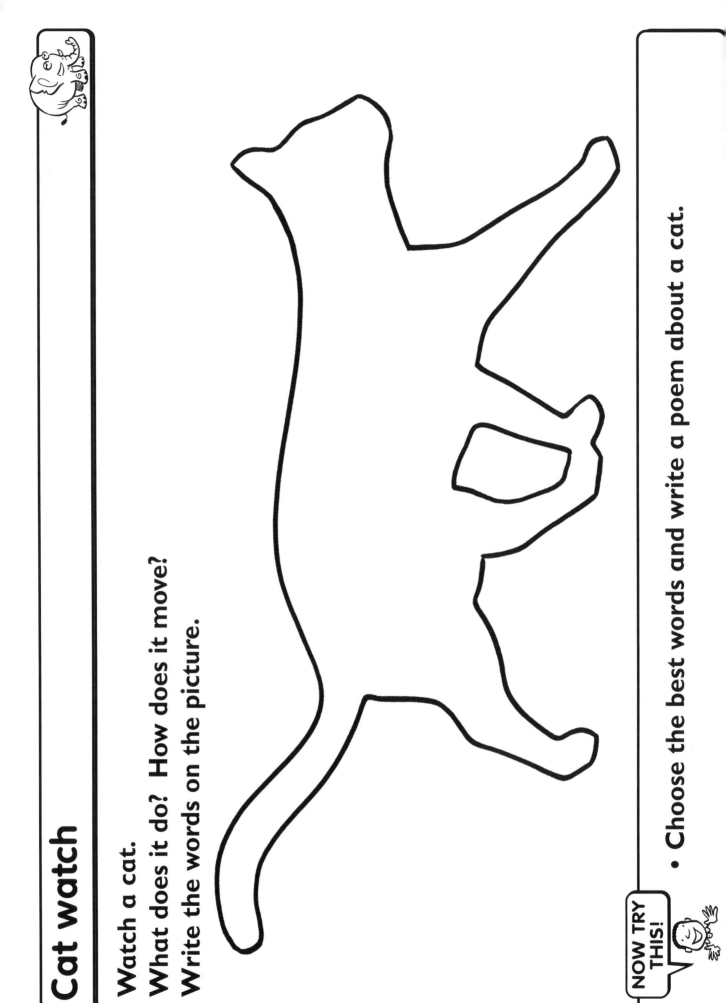

- Watch a cat.
- What does it do? How does it move?
- Write the words on the picture.

- Choose the best words and write a poem about a cat.

Teachers' note If possible let the children watch a real cat. Otherwise they could watch a video of a cat moving. Invite them to talk about how it moves and to suggest words for this. You could supply words to help them, such as *slink, creep, pad, tiptoe, silent, softly, smoothly, graceful, nimble.*

A Lesson for Every Day
Literacy
6–7 Years
© A&C Black

Rain

- **On a rainy day**
  - – watch
  - – listen
  - – feel.

- **On the splashes, write words for what you**
  - – see
  - – hear
  - – feel.

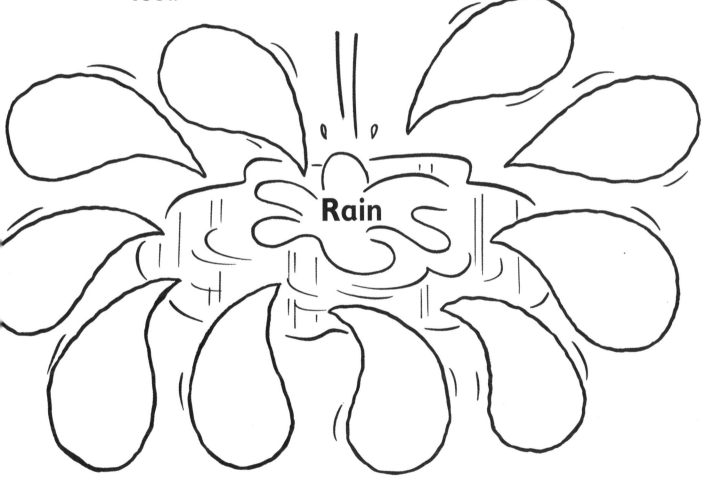

Rain

NOW TRY THIS!

- **Use the words in a poem about rain.**

Teachers' note Use this page on a rainy day. The children could go outside to observe the rain. Record the words they use to talk about what they see, hear and feel. Back in class they can write the best ones on the splashes.

A Lesson for Every Day
Literacy
6-7 Years
© A&C Black

Sounds right

- **What are the people saying?**
- **Write the words in the speech bubbles.**
- **Say the words aloud with a partner.**

Use expression.

Quick! He's coming! Hide in here.	Come into my house, children. I have lots of sweets.
Who's been eating my dinner?	Don't you ever do that again.

NOW TRY THIS!

- **Read a short story aloud.**
- **Change your voice for each character.**

Use expression.

Teachers' note At the start of the lesson, read the story of Snow White with the children (not just the Disney version), to ensure that they know the dwarf's response. Before writing in the speech bubbles the children could enact the scenes in the pictures with a friend and say the words in an appropriate tone of voice, using appropriate facial expressions, hands, body language and actions

A Lesson for Every Day
Literacy
6-7 Years
© A&C Black

Fixing the wheels on

- **How can you fix on the wheels?**
- **Choose the materials you need.**
- **Talk about how to use them.**
- **Write what you agree to do.**

Work with a group.

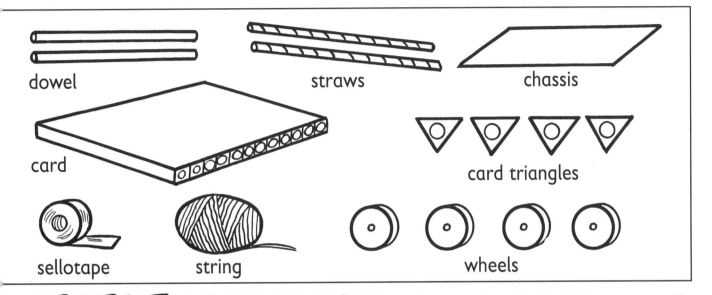

dowel
straws
chassis
card
card triangles
sellotape
string
wheels

What we need

What we shall do

NOW TRY THIS!

- **Try your idea.**

Teachers' note The children should look at and use the materials depicted: wooden dowel, art straw or wide drinking straws, 'Correx' card, card triangles, sellotape, string and wooden wheels. Ask them whether the axles need to be able to turn and, if so, whether the wheels should turn on the axles or be fixed to them (show them examples on model or toy cars).

A Lesson for Every Day
Literacy
6–7 Years
© A&C Black

All in all

- **Read the messages.**
- **Rewrite them with a word that starts** `al` .

We can go to the beach.
We can go to the fair, _too_.

We can go to the beach.
We can go to the fair, also.

It's <u>nearly</u> time
to go home.

It's _____ time to go
home.

There are six sweets in one
box and ten in the other.
That's sixteen <u>in all</u>.

_____

_____

_____

Hello Jake.
Are you <u>OK</u>?

_____

_____

When we play, he cheats.
<u>Every time</u>.

_____

_____

_____

<u>Even though</u> he was tired,
he finished the race.

_____

_____

NOW TRY THIS!

- **Write a sentence using** `already` .

Teachers' note Remind the children of their previous learning about the letters used for spelling the /or/ phoneme and that **al** can be used to spell /or/ in a few words. For a less challenging activity, provide a word-bank: _almost, alright, also, although, altogether, always._

A Lesson for Every Day
Literacy
6-7 Years
© A&C Black

Word addition

- **Add a word from the word-bank.**
- **Read the new word.**

Word-bank

ball	crow	end	head	nut	sun
bell	door	foot	house	shine	tale

light_____

_____mat

_____ache

snow_____

fairy_____

week_____

_____print

_____light

pea_____

door_____

sun_____

scare_____

NOW TRY THIS!

- **Write a word in the gap to make a long word.**

_____lash   motor_____   _____mill

sea_____   jelly_____   bed_____

out_____   farm_____   _____stool

Teachers' note Remind the children of compound words they have formed before. Model the first example by reading the word *light* aloud and then reading it with each word from the list in turn: *Lightball – No, that's not a word; Lightbell – No, that's not a word*, until you reach *house: Lighthouse – Yes, that's a word*. Complete the new word *lighthouse* and cross out *house* in the word-bank.

A Lesson for Every Day
Literacy
6-7 Years
© A&C Black

207

Wild words

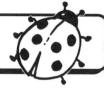

- ## Finish the pairs of words.

The first sounds must be the same.

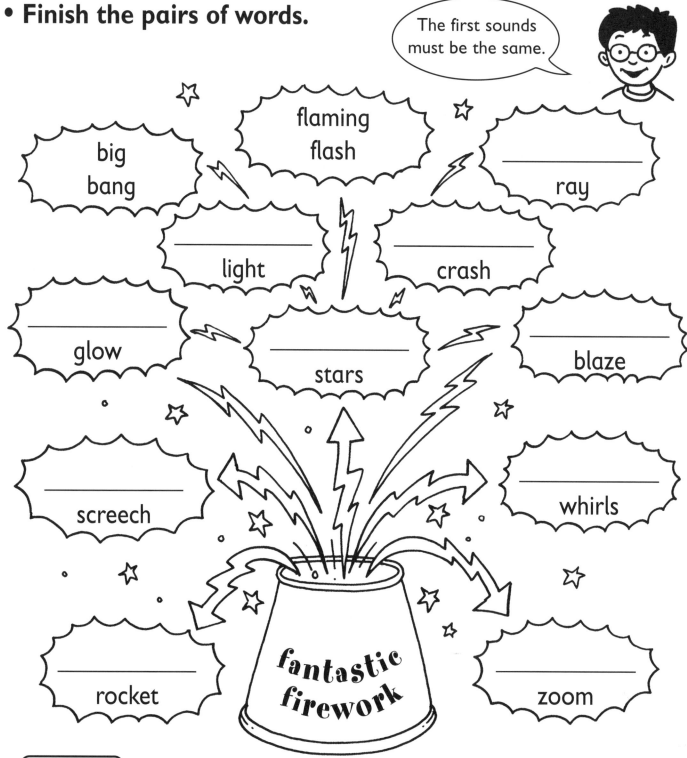

big
bang

flaming
flash

_____
ray

_____
light

_____
crash

_____
glow

_____
stars

_____
blaze

_____
screech

fantastic firework

_____
whirls

_____
rocket

_____
zoom

NOW TRY THIS!

- ## Make up some word-pairs about snow.
Example: floating flakes

208

Teachers' note Say a few alliterative phrases and ask the children what they notice about the sounds: for example, *fuzzy felt, flip-flops, zig-zag*. Read some poems containing alliteration and point out how this can create an effect such as silence, a rough sea and so on. Encourage the children to think of words which help to create an effect, such as *whizzing whirls, crunching crash, gleaming glow*.

A Lesson for Every Day
Literacy
6-7 Years
© A&C Black

A funny little man

- **Think of words to write in the gaps.**
- **Write the words.**
- **Read the poem with a friend.**

Dan, Dan, the funny little man,
Washed his face in the frying pan,
Combed his hair with the leg of the chair,
Dan, Dan, the funny little man.

Dan, Dan, the funny little man,
Brushed his teeth with a _____,
Blew his nose with _____,
Dan, Dan, the funny little man.

Dan, Dan, the funny little man,
Cleaned his shoes with a _____,
Washed his shirt in _____,
Dan, Dan, the funny little man.

Dan, Dan, the funny little man,
Washed his car with a _____,
Shaved his face with _____,
Dan, Dan, the funny little man.

NOW TRY THIS!

- **Make up a verse for a poem about a silly teacher.**

Teachers' note Allow the children time to read the poem with a friend and have fun trying out different words in the gaps: for example, *brushed his teeth with a leg of lamb, blew his nose with the garden hose, cleaned his shoes with a slice of ham, washed his shirt in a bowl of dirt, washed his car with a bucket of bran, shaved his face with a piece of plaice.*

A Lesson for Every Day
Literacy
6-7 Years
© A&C Black

Mrs Brown went to town

- ## Sing the first verse about Mrs Brown.
- ## Write three new verses.
- ## Sing your poem.

Mrs Brown went to town,
Riding on a pony,
When she came back she lost her hat,
And called on Miss Maloney.

Mrs Brown went to town,
Riding on a push-bike,
When she came back she lost her hat,
And called on _____.

Mrs Brown went to town,
Riding on a tandem,
When she came back she lost her hat,
And called on _____.

Mrs Brown went to town,
Driving a Mercedes,
When she came back she lost her hat,
And called on _____.

NOW TRY THIS!

- ## Make up a verse about a man who went to war.

Teachers' note Sing the first verse with the children to the tune of *Yankee Doodle*, then let them sing the rest with their friends, making up the missing parts. Stop them at intervals and invite volunteers to sing a verse to the class. They can then choose the versions they want to write. You could write this or key it as a display to which the children could add new verses (perhaps on a 'graffiti wall').

A Lesson for Every Day
Literacy
6-7 Years
© A&C Black

Tongue-twister match-up

Beginnings	**Endings**

Lesley licked a yellow lolly;

the fritters Fred fried were fine.

Fred fried four fritters;

the dishes Dizzy Dora dropped were dusty.

William wore red wellies;

the lolly Lesley licked was yellow.

Terry tried to taste the treacle;

in Shelly's silly shoe shop.

Shelly sold silly shoes;

and William waded in the river.

Dizzy Dora dropped the dishes;

the treacle trickled down Terry's trousers.

Gordon Green grows ghosts in his garden;

the best bananas are bent by Ben.

Ben Bone bends bananas;

Gordon grins as the ghosts grow.

Teachers' note Cut out the beginnings and the endings or ask the children to do so and they can then match up each beginning with an ending. Or give each child a beginning or an ending and ask them to read them aloud and find their partners.

A Lesson for Every Day
Literacy
6–7 Years
© A&C Black

Tongue-twisters

- **Finish the tongue-twisters.**
- **Read them aloud quickly.**

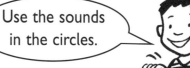 Use the sounds in the circles.

Example: Carla crunched crisps
In the corner of the class.

 c   cr   cl

 William went to Rome

_____ .

 w   r

 Tracy tastes a treacle tart

_____ .

 t   tr

 Kit kissed Kitty quite quickly

_____ .

k   q

c

 Twenty tiny twigs twisted in a tree

_____ .

 t   tr

tw

 Gary grabbed a green glass

_____ .

 g   gr

gl

NOW TRY THIS!

- **Write a tongue-twister using these sounds.** l r

 212

Teachers' note The children first need to read some tongue-twisters and to notice the sounds that cause the difficulties. Read the example tongue-twister with them – at first slowly and then increasingly quickly. Point out that sounds that are similar are hard to read quickly one after the other and that people usually mix them up.

A Lesson for Every Day
Literacy
6-7 Years
© A&C Black

Riddles

Write a riddle to spell star .
Make up a clue for the last line.

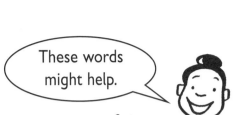

These words might help.

back	face	locket	race	socket
cat	fly	my	rack	space
cot	fry	night	rice	spice
cry	high	pack	rocket	tea
diamond	lace	pie	sea	track
dry	like	pocket	sight	twinkle

My first is in *space* but not in _____

My second is in _____

_____

My third is in _____

_____

My fourth is in _____

_____

_____

_____

NOW TRY THIS!

- **Write a riddle for another word.**
- **Give it to a friend to solve.**

Teachers' note Read some riddles with the children and demonstrate how they give the reader clues about something and often help to spell the answer.

A Lesson for Every Day
Literacy
6-7 Years
© A&C Black

Ask a silly question

- **Write the answers in the speech bubbles.**
- **Read the questions and answers with a friend.**

What makes grass dangerous?

The blades!

What does a fish use for weighing?

Which part of a comb bites?

Which part of a plant helps you to see in the dark?

What kind of singer twinkles?

Which part of a window is sore?

- **Write silly questions and answers about these.**

| an ear of corn | a jumper | a wave in the sea |

Teachers' note Read and discuss the first question and answer with the children. Ask them why the answer is *blades*. Where have they seen a blade? If necessary, explain that the name given to a spike of grass is called a *blade*. Point out that blade has two meanings and discuss the questions and the two meanings of the words in the word-bank.

A Lesson for Every Day
Literacy
6-7 Years
© A&C Black

Silly birthdays

- **Make up some silly Happy Birthday songs.**
- **Sing them with a friend.**

The rhyme-bank will help.

> Happy birthday to you!
> Squashed tomatoes and stew
> Eggs and bacon for breakfast
> Happy birthday to you!

Rhyme-bank
blue blew
crew drew do
few flew 'flu
glue goo grew
moo new knew
pew screw shoe
to too two
true through
view who
you zoo

Happy birthday to you!

_____

_____

_____

Happy birthday to you!

_____

_____

_____

NOW TRY THIS!

- **Do your new lines have the right number of beats?**
- **Change them if you need to.**

Teachers' note The children could first sing the silly Happy birthday song shown here. They may well know it already. Ask them which words rhyme and note that they are at the ends of lines. They can then use the words in the rhyme-bank to help them to make up other silly Happy birthday songs, which they could sing during the plenary session.

A Lesson for Every Day
Literacy
6–7 Years
© A&C Black

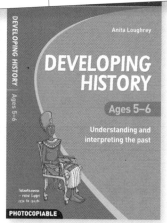
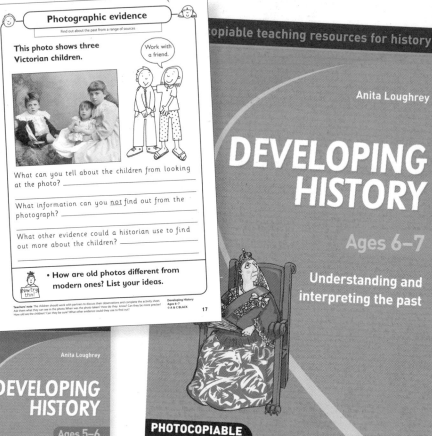
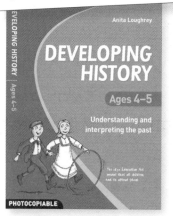
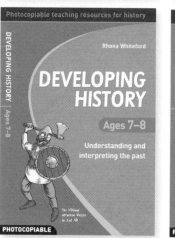
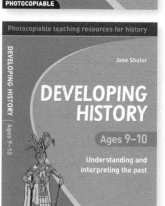
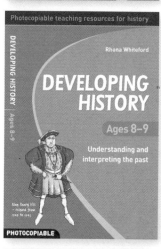
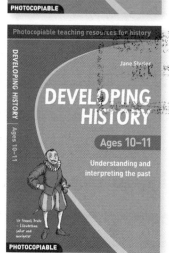